THE ECONOMICS OF SOVIET BREAK-UP

Before 1991, little was written or known of the individual states which made up the USSR, and their identities were subsumed into the Russian monolith. *The Economics of Soviet Break-up* analyses the effects of the break-up of the Soviet Union into fifteen independent states. Topics discussed include:

- past and present economic relations between the republics, and forecasts for the future;
- discussion of Customs Unions, Monetary Union or a Payments Union as possible ways forward for these states;
- economic integration theory;
- how the states of the Soviet Union functioned before the dissolution.

This up-to-date study is based on original research and extensive travel in the former Soviet Union. It meets an urgent need for information about this important subject and will be of interest to all students of the economics, politics and recent history of the Soviet republics.

Bert van Selm is a Lecturer at the Institute of East European Law and Russian Studies, University of Leiden. He has written numerous journal articles on the economics of the Soviet break-up, and has travelled widely through the former USSR.

ROUTLEDGE STUDIES OF SOCIETIES
IN TRANSITION

1. THE ECONOMICS OF SOVIET BREAK-UP
Bert van Selm

THE ECONOMICS OF SOVIET BREAK-UP

Bert van Selm

ROUTLEDGE

London and New York

First published 1997
by Routledge
11 New Fetter Lane, London, EC4P 4EE

Simultaneously published in the USA and Canada
by Routledge
29 West 35th Street, New York, NY 10001

© 1997 Bert van Selm

Typeset in Garamond by
J&L Composition Ltd, Filey, North Yorkshire

Printed and bound in Great Britain by
Creative Print and Design (Wales), Ebbw Vale

British Library Cataloguing in Publication Data
A catalogue record for this book is available from
the British Library

Library of Congress Cataloging in Publication Data
Selm, B. van
The economics of Soviet break-up/Bert van Selm.
Includes bibliographical references and index.
1. Post-communism—Economic aspects—Former
Soviet republics.   2. Former Soviet republics—Economic
integration.   3. Former Soviet republics—
Economic conditions.   I. Title.
HC336.27.S45   1997
338.947—dc20   96–36174

ISBN 0–415–14832–4

CONTENTS

CONTENTS

TABLES

TABLES

PREFACE

This book was written from 1990 to 1995, a time span that could have been the period of the thirteenth *pyatiletka* of the Soviet Union (the twelfth and last was from 1985 to 1990). During this interval things changed rapidly in the East. I started off working on a thesis under the title 'Costs and Benefits of Independence for the Baltic Republics', and I remember a few birthday parties at which the relevance of such a study was questioned; the topic was considered highly academic. But time was on my side, and by the end of 1991 the Soviet Union had ceased to exist.

I used five winters to read, think and write at my desk in Groningen. The summers I spent travelling in the (former) Soviet Union. I was in Moscow and Suchumi in 1990, in Petersburg, Riga and Vilnious in 1991, in Moscow and Kiev in 1992, on the Volga and in Yalta in 1993, and in Odessa in 1994. The general impression of these successive visits was one of increasing chaos, poverty, inequality, violence and crime. Suchumi was besieged and taken by Abchaz forces in 1993, and today it is not visited by Western scholars, but by CIS peacekeepers. The changes in Moscow over the last couple of years have been equally devastating. In 1993, I had dinner one evening in the 'Aist' ('Stork'). A week later, a mafioso entered this restaurant, emptied his submachine gun on the guests, killing two, and then ran off, pitching a hand grenade in the place as a farewell present. Such an event would have been unthinkable in 1990. Let us hope this trend does not lend itself to extrapolation (I am afraid it does).

Of all the people who in one way or another contributed to this work, I want to single out two. The first is my dear friend Emiel Dölle. Many of the initial ideas were his (such as the idea for Chapter 5, worked out three years later) and some parts of this book were written in very close cooperation (Chapter 8 is an example). Together we attended seminars in Göttingen, Trento and Brussels, made endless train trips through Russia and the Ukraine, swam in the Don and in the Black Sea, and dreamt of fortunes via *Oostenwindhandel VoF.* Yes, those were the days.

Even more important were the contributions of Hans-Jürgen Wagener. A PhD student cannot possibly wish for a more stimulating, quick-reading, interested and dedicated professor. We co-authored Chapters 4 and 7, and his comments have improved the quality of all other chapters immeasurably. I can only hope that this book succeeds to some extent in fulfilling the promise implicit in the title of his 1972 book *Ansätze zu einer Regionanalyse der Sowjetunion.*

Thanks are also due to Wladimir Andreff, Willem Buiter, Leendert Colijn, Bruno Dallago, Geske Dijkstra, Henk de Haan, Herman Hoen, Ger Lanjouw, Beppo van Leeuwen and Joanne Thorburn for their valuable comments on the manuscript or part of it; and to Boudewijn Berendsen, Klaas Knot, Fieke van der Lecq and Stefan Lerz for being good office mates. For financial support I thank the Dutch organisation for Scientific Research (NWO).

Bert van Selm
Leiden, 1996

ACKNOWLEDGEMENTS

This book is largely based on a number of articles that have appeared in journals and a book over the last few years. These articles are:

'Former Soviet Republics' Economic Interdependence', *Osteuropa Wirtschaft*, 1993, no.1, pp.23–39 (with H.-J. Wagener).

'Soviet Interrepublican Capital Transfers and the Republics' Level of Development, 1966–91', in *MOST. Economic Journal on Eastern Europe and the Former Soviet Union*, 1993, no.1, pp.133–49 (with E. Dölle).

'Integration and Disintegration in Europe: EC versus Former USSR', in G. Pegoretti and B. Dallago eds, *Integration and Disintegration in Europe: Divergent or Convergent Processes*, Dartmouth, Aldershot, 1995, pp.93–112.

'A Gravity Model of the Former Soviet Union', *Journal of International and Comparative Economics*, 1995, no.1, pp. 61–9.

'The Economics of Soviet Break-up', *Ukrainian Economic Review*, 1995, no.1–2, pp. 79–95.

'The CIS Payments Union: A Post-Mortem', *MOST. Economic Journal on Eastern Europe and the Former Soviet Union*, 1995, no.3, pp. 25–36 (with H.-J. Wagener).

Thanks are due to the publishers of the journals and the book for granting permission for 'updated republication'.

1

INTRODUCTION AND
OVERVIEW

This study is an enquiry into *the economic effects of the break-up of the Soviet Union* into fifteen independent states.

The economic effects? Surely we do not claim to capture all. One of the economic effects of Soviet break-up is for example a sharp reduction in the Dutch defence budget. But we are not primarily interested in the Dutch defence budget here. We concentrate on the effects that Soviet break-up has on the economies of the Newly Independent States. Of these effects, we pick out those that we consider most important from an *economic* point of view. A very important effect of Soviet break-up is that one nuclear state has quadrupled into four: the Russian Federation, Belarus, Kazakhstan and Ukraine. We do not analyse the (undoubtedly detrimental) effects on world security of this nuclear break-up. Ukraine's nuclear weapons come in only as an exchange for Russian oil. By *break-up* we mean the division of a single state into a number of smaller states. As such, break-up is not related to the demise of Communism and the transition from a planned economy to a market economy. Of course, the USSR would not have broken up without this demise, but that is another story. Finally, we put some emphasis on the Soviet *Union*. We concentrate on the role of the USSR as a union of fifteen republics. Chapters 3, 4 and 5 describe the Soviet Union, the republics and the economic interaction among them. In this overview and Chapter 2, we concentrate on the economic effects of break-up.

Break-up means that new borders are created. If borders were irrelevant from an economic point of view, there would be no economics of break-up, and this would be the end of the story. So first we turn to the 'Border Irrelevance Proposition'. According to the 'neoclassical theory of political boundaries', the exact form of

1

the boundaries between nations is intrinsically unimportant for long-run economic performance. This proposition, to be scrutinised in Chapter 2, applies strictly to a 'nonmonetary economy characterised by perfect competition, private ownership of all commodities, free trade, and no income redistribution by the government' (Nordhaus *et al.* 1991: 322). Of course, few 'really existing' economies are adequately characterised in this way, and certainly not the Soviet Union. Let us briefly consider each of the qualifications in turn.

John Maynard Keynes singled out free trade as the most important of the conditions under which borders are irrelevant from an economic point of view:

> In a regime of free trade and free economic intercourse it would be of little consequences that iron lay on one side of a political frontier, and labour, coal and blast furnaces on the other. But as it is, men have devised ways to impoverish themselves and one another; and prefer collective animosities to individual happiness.
>
> (Keynes 1919: 99)

If goods (iron and coal) and production factors (labour and capital in the blast furnace) can move freely, the economic significance of a border is greatly reduced.

A union of states that allows goods to move freely among the participating members is a free trade area or, if they have a common external trade policy, a *Customs Union*. If a group of states agrees to allow the free mobility of labour and capital among them on top of the free mobility of goods, it is called a *Common Market*. Here we suppose that within a state goods and factors can move freely. By implication, if a state breaks up, an effect of this could be that goods and factors can no longer move freely. It all depends on whether or not the newly formed states agree to form a Customs Union or a Common Market.

In the case of the Soviet Union, this effect of break-up is strong and important. Goods and factors used to be highly mobile between the republics before 1991. By 1994, mobility had been reduced drastically. No functioning Customs Union or Common Market among the fifteen has been created, and the chances of this happening in the near future are small. We apply in Chapter 6 economic theory on Customs Unions to assess whether the formation of such an institution among the fifteen would be desirable or not.

The second qualification to the 'Border Irrelevance Proposition' is that it applies only to a non-monetary economy. Even though the rouble has often been criticised for not properly fulfilling the traditional functions of money, especially that of a means of exchange, calling the Soviet Union a non-monetary economy would certainly go too far. The fifteen republics shared a common rouble. More generally, states usually have a single currency, and hence also a single monetary policy and a single exchange rate. Break-up opens up the possibility of introducing new currencies, to have different monetary policies and different exchange rates. Of course, the new states can decide to fix their exchange rates and coordinate their monetary policies, or even decide to create a common currency (a *Monetary Union*), as the EU member states have done. As in the case of goods and factor mobility, the creation of a border need not have economic implications. However, Soviet break-up has had important monetary consequences. The shared rouble is history now. Chapter 6 is about the Soviet Union as a Monetary Union, and about the desirability of creating a new common currency or fixing exchange rates.

Next, income redistribution should be absent if the 'Border Irrelevance Proposition' is to hold. This qualification is about as implausible as the previous one. States redistribute among their citizens and among their regions in many ways, sometimes explicitly but more often implicitly. For example, progressive income taxation is an implicit way of redistributing wealth from rich parts of the state to poor parts. Regional development funds are an explicit redistribution mechanism.

Redistribution exists not only *within* states, but also *between* states. Development aid is an obvious example. However, the scale of redistribution between parts of a state is very different from redistribution between states. Rich states seldom donate more than 1 per cent of their GNP to poor states, and poor states seldom receive more than 5 per cent of *their* GNP. Conversely, donating or receiving 10 per cent or more is not unusual for a region. For example, in 1972 Bretagne received 11 per cent of its GNP from the rest of France, in the years 1971 to 1973 Lombardia donated 11 per cent of its GNP to the rest of Italy, in 1964 Northern Ireland received 16.1 per cent of its GNP from the rest of the United Kingdom, and from 1971 to 1973 Calabria received 23.5 per cent of its GNP as a donation from the rest of Italy (CEC 1977: 33). The huge transfers from the western to the eastern German *Länder* after reunification in 1990 are a more recent example. The reason for this difference in magnitude lies in a difference in mechanism. Within states, implicit redistribution is more important, whereas between states explicit redistribution is the main mechanism. In Chapter 8, we show that redistribution flows among the fifteen republics were very significant in the former Soviet Union. Conversely, future redistribution among the Newly Independent States can be expected to be limited. This is an important aspect of Soviet break-up.

Finally we come to the last qualification to the 'Border Irrelevance Proposition': perfect competition and private ownership. Again this is a heroic assumption. Private ownership certainly cannot be taken for granted. Instead, the relative size of private property to public property is (at least partly) determined by the economic system that is chosen by the state. If the state opts for a Communist-type economy, the means of production are not private, but public. States matter because they choose their preferred economic system. More relevant in the case of the Soviet Union, states matter because they choose the speed and the method of the *transition* to their preferred system. Break-up enables the Newly Independent States to have their own stabilisation and privatisation policies, for example. This is the topic of Chapter 9.

To recapitulate, we have thus far found four reasons why political borders and states matter from an economic point of view. They do because:

1 A state is a Customs Union.
2 A state is a Monetary Union.
3 A state is a redistributor.
4 A state is a system elector.

As a first exercise in the economics of break-up, let us apply this framework of analysis to the closest historical precedent that we have at hand, which is the break-up of the Austro-Hungarian empire. As in the case of the Soviet Union, a single unit of adjacent territories broke up into a number of independent states. The treaties drafted at the 1919 Paris Conference divided the territory of the old empire among two existing states (Italy and Romania) and five new ones (Austria, Czechoslovakia, Hungary, Yugoslavia,

INTRODUCTION AND OVERVIEW

Poland; the first three were fully within the borders of the prewar empire). The Austro-Hungarian empire was characterised by:

1 No internal barriers to trade.
2 A single currency – the Austrian crown.
3 Redistribution via fiscal cooperation – each of the two constituent parts of the empire had its own budget. However, common expenses were paid out of customs receipts and contributions from the two regional governments. Under the terms of the last prewar agreement, Austria paid 63.6 per cent of the residual common expenditures. The terms of these budget agreements, including the tariff structure and the distribution of the expenses between the two states, were to be renegotiated every ten years (Garber and Spencer 1994: 2).
4 A market economy.

After break-up,

> within a matter of months, a monetary and customs union of 68 years standing had been dissolved, and the successor republics of the Empire were printing their own currencies and implementing stringent controls over trade across their borders.
>
> (de Ménil and Maurel 1994: 553)

The fiscal unity broke down; fortunately none of the successor states introduced a planned economy, even though the introduction of some form of socialism was discussed in Vienna in 1919. The combined effects of these changes on economic performance were negative. Growth in the successor states stagnated, and inflation ran high. In the years following World War I, prices increased in Austria by 1,400,000 per cent; in Hungary by 2,300,000 per cent; Yugoslavia, 990 per cent; Romania, 4,111 per cent; Poland, 250,000,000 per cent (Nordhaus *et al.* 1991: 326–7). Only Czechoslovakia managed to stabilise its newly introduced currency and its price level quickly, but the price paid was very high in terms of unemployment (Dornbusch 1992: 402). Break-up was perceived by the new states as the main cause of their economic trouble. Plans for a Danubian Economic Union were made, and conferences were held, but no progress was made (Dornbusch 1992: 417). Trade among the parts of the former empire was sharply reduced (for some empirical evidence, see de Ménil and Maurel 1994: 555).

The dismal story of the Austro-Hungarian break-up might tempt one to conclude that the economics of break-up are negative for all parties concerned, and hence also for the whole. Pity the town of Lvov that lay both in the Austro-Hungarian and the 'Evil Empire' and is today once again experiencing break-up. Yet this conclusion is by no means necessarily valid. The combined welfare of the regions involved is not necessarily reduced by break-up, and may even increase as a result of it. This is all the more true for the parts of the whole:

1 The notion that world welfare is maximised under world free trade is part of the economist's creed. Yet, as Viner first showed half a century ago, removing some barriers to trade while leaving others unchanged might only make things worse (Chapter 6 makes clear why and how). Customs Unions can be welfare decreasing for all parties concerned. States are Customs Unions. By implication, states can be welfare decreasing for all parties (regions, provinces, etc.) concerned.

2 Worldwide free trade may still be part of all economists' creeds, worldwide fixed exchange rates are certainly not. Instead, the idea behind the notion of 'optimum currency areas' is that parts of the world differ from one another, that these differences are changing over time, and that therefore it might be handy to have the possibility to change the exchange between these areas to accommodate such changes (the theory of monetary unions is discussed at length in Chapter 6). States are currency areas. They may be optimal, but they also may not be. Therefore the combined welfare of the regions could increase if the state that unites these regions breaks up. From the point of view of a part of the whole, the advantage of breaking up a monetary union is that an instrument of economic policy is gained. In a state that has an oil-producing region, for example, other regions might suffer from an overvalued exchange rate that is caused by huge oil exports (in other words, the 'Dutch Disease' often has a regional aspect). If such a state breaks up, this opens up the possibility for the non-oil regions to devalue.

3 Redistribution is by definition welfare neutral on the union level, but not on the level of the constituent parts. The break-up of states does not change the combined welfare of the parts involved because of the role of the state as a redistributor, but it is likely to increase the welfare of some regions and reduce that of

others. Usually break-up would increase the welfare of the rich regions and reduce that of the poor on account of redistribution, as in the cases of Slovenia and the Czech Republic for example. The example of the Soviet Union in Chapter 8 makes clear that this is not necessarily true.

4 Finally, break-up can be an advantage to parts of the whole if the whole was not very good at transforming its economy from a planned to a market economy. In the case of the USSR there was certainly room for improvement over perestroika policies and, after 1991, room for improvement over Russian transition policies, as Chapter 9 makes clear.

In summary, break-up may be likely to be a negative sum game as in the case of Austria–Hungary, but it is not necessarily so and it may even be a positive sum game. Break-up has many different economic effects, and for the parties concerned some are likely to be welfare increasing and others welfare reducing. Assessing the net effect of break-up on a region may be very hard, if not impossible. The reader should not expect a listing at the end of this book of the fifteen former Soviet republics with the gains or losses of break-up calculated for each in billion dollars. This study cannot be more than a small contribution to a highly complicated subject. We consider it a success if we succeed in doing just that.

Once it is clear that some parts might gain from break-up, the question of whether economic factors may have been conducive to break-up follows naturally. Great prudence is required here. The driving force behind the break-up of both Austria–Hungary and the Soviet Union was not economics, but nationalism. Nevertheless, economic aspects do seem to have at least some relevance in the latter case. One of the conclusions of this study is that for the three Baltic republics of the Soviet Union, break-up had at least some positive economic effects, mainly connected with the role of the state as a system elector. Conversely, for the five Central Asian republics finding a positive economic effect of break-up is difficult, the main disadvantages being related to the role of the state as a redistributor. The temptation to link this result to the fact that the Baltic republics could not wait to leave the Soviet Union, whereas the moves of the Central Asian republics over the last couple of years were slow, is too great for us to resist, and seems more plausible than the alternative explanation for the difference in their behaviour, i.e. that Balts are more nationalistic than Central Asians.

In this book, however, we concentrate on the economic *effects* of the creation of political borders, without analysing economic *causes* of political border creation.

We assume and hope that Soviet break-up continues to be a relatively peaceful event. In the case of the Yugoslavian break-up, talking about the economic aspects of the matter seems improper. The remaining relative peace in the Soviet case is by no means certain. States hardly ever break up without violence. Belgian secession from Holland in 1830 is often presented as an example of an orderly split, but even the Netherlands had its 'ten-day campaign'. If break-up is violent, some parties may win militarily, but all lose economically, and break-up is clearly a negative sum game.

ORGANISATION OF THIS BOOK

The central question of the study, *Do borders matter?*, is addressed by taking Nordhaus *et al.*'s 'Border Irrelevance Proposition' as a benchmark. We use this proposition to draw up a checklist of potential economic effects from political break-up in *Chapter 2*. This checklist is the basis for the rest of the book. We describe some historical, demographic, juridical, geographic, and cultural aspects of the Soviet Union in *Chapter 3*. The existing level of economic integration at the time of break-up is the subject of *Chapter 4*. By applying a gravity model, further information about the internal cohesion of the Soviet economy is obtained in *Chapter 5*. Subsequently this model is applied to estimate future trade flows among the republics. The latter indicator is important in the subsequent chapter, when we discuss the costs and benefits of a Customs Union and a Monetary Union (*Chapter 6*) among the Newly Independent States. An important effect of the creation of a political frontier is that the constituent parts of the union are no longer automatically in a Customs Union or a Monetary Union. If the Monetary Union breaks up, a Payments Union could be considered as an alternative. This is the subject of *Chapter 7*. Another important effect of political break-up is the disappearance of a single state budget through which redistribution takes place. This is analysed for the Soviet Union in *Chapter 8*. Finally, political independence enables the republics to follow their own road to market. A comparative study of the transition strategies in the Newly Independent States is therefore taken up in *Chapter 9*. *Chapter 10* pulls all the lines of the analysis together.

2

THE ECONOMICS OF SOVIET
BREAK-UP

This chapter analyses the economic consequences of the creation of new political borders. Taking Nordhaus *et al.*'s 'Border Irrelevance Proposition' as a benchmark, a checklist of potential economic effects from political break-up is drawn up. Subsequently we apply this list to the break-up of the Soviet Union.

A PROPOSITION

The idea that borders do not — or at least need not — really matter from an economic point of view has some history in economic writings. In one book on the subject, E.A.G. Robinson's *Economic Consequences of the Size of Nations*, we read that

> Some political units which may be juridically entitled to be called nations are so effectively integrated into larger economies that the degree of real discontinuity is negligible: Monaco, for example, or Andorra, or the Vatican City. Indeed, the concept of a nation would be largely irrelevant from the point of view of economic analysis if everywhere all that is practicable were done to minimize discontinuities and to promote mobility.
>
> (Robinson 1960: xiv)

This 'Border Irrelevance Proposition' has recently been repeated by Nordhaus *et al.*:

> According to the neoclassical theory of political boundaries, the exact form of the boundaries between nations is intrinsically unimportant for long-run economic performance. The precise proposition is that the average income in a region is, to

9

a first approximation, unaffected by the placement of boundary lines in that region. From an analytical point of view, this proposition rests on standard neoclassical analysis and applies strictly to a (1) nonmonetary economy characterised by (2) perfect competition, (3) private ownership of all commodities, (4) free trade, and (5) no income redistribution by the government. In other words, if we examine a standard general equilibrium model with free trade, the outcome (in terms of prices, incomes, and outputs) is independent of whether the different commodities are identified as American, Soviet, Russian, or Kirgiz.

(Nordhaus *et al.* 1991: 322; numbers in brackets added)

This paragraph suggests that there exists a certain literature on the 'neoclassical theory of political boundaries' and that a precise proposition concerning the economic relevance of political boundaries is written down somewhere in that literature. After some fruitless library research I wrote a letter to Nordhaus asking for further references. This is the reply I received:

Dear Mr. van Selm,

I am afraid that there are no references to what we call the 'boundary irrelevance proposition', but I believe that it is an obvious proposition in neoclassical economics. The reasoning is that patterns of relative prices, outputs, consumption, trade, and productivity are determined solely by tastes and technology in a neoclassical market economy of the Arrow-Debreu type. There is no money or trade barriers, zoning or regulations, taxes or transfers, and therefore there is no role for political boundaries. Incidentally, the proposition is clearly wrong in reality, but it is for reasons other than the ones associated with competitive markets.

Sincerely yours, William D. Nordhaus

It seems that the 'neoclassical theory of political boundaries' is desperately in need of some theorising. Let us examine more closely each of the conditions mentioned by Nordhaus *et al.* in their original formulation. The exact proposition under consideration is that a political border between two states has no bearing on either their aggregate wealth (the 'pie'), or the distribution of it.

First, we must define precisely what we mean by 'state' or 'political border'. In this book, a circular definition is used to discriminate between states and non-states. A state is a territory that has been accepted by the other states as a state. The advantage of this definition is that it is very operational. A territory is a state only if the United Nations have accepted it as a state. Thus in 1994 Tadzjikistan is a state, but Tatarstan is not. A 'political border' is then the line that separates two adjacent territories that have both been accepted as states. 'Break-up' is the creation of these 'political borders'. 'Soviet break-up' is the creation of 'political borders' in a territory that used to be a single state, the Soviet Union.

Next, let us consider a hypothetical world that consists of two hypothetical states, 'Holland' and 'Belgium'. 'Belgium' consists of two parts, 'Flanders' and 'Wallonia'. Suppose Belgium breaks up, and both Flanders and Wallonia are promoted to the status of state. Nordhaus *et al.*'s proposition claims that this political event has no effects either on the combined wealth of Flanders and Wallonia or on the distribution of this wealth between the two if:

1 Belgium, Flanders, Wallonia and Holland are non-monetary economies. This assumption is unduly strong. Surely there would be no monetary consequences from the Belgian break-up if all parties concerned were non-monetary economies, but the same is true if Flanders and Wallonia stick to the Belgian monetary arrangements. If we assume that states have one currency at maximum and do not allow their constituent parts to run their own monies (plausible enough for twentieth century states), this implies that after break-up Flanders and Wallonia should have a common currency, and that this currency should have the same relation to the Dutch guilder as the old Belgian franc.

2 Perfect competition should characterise the economies of Belgium, Flanders and Wallonia. Is that really necessary? Suppose the Belgian economy consisted purely of duopolies: every Flemish firm had its competitor in Wallonia and vice versa. If Belgium breaks up and prohibitive trade barriers are installed, this implies that the degree of monopolisation of both the Flemish and the Wallonian economy rises to 100 per cent, with all the detrimental effects connected. But if free trade between Flanders and Wallonia is allowed, the presence or absence of perfect competition does not make any difference. Thus 2 is not a necessary condition. The correct formulation is that an unfulfilled condition (2) increases the effects of an unfulfilled condi-

11

tion (4). It seems that both conditions 1 and 2 are given here not because they are necessary conditions for a 'Border Irrelevance Proposition' to hold, but rather because they are part of standard neoclassical analysis.

3 All Belgian, Flemish and Wallonian property should be private. Unfortunately, this condition renders the proposition a tautology (another familiar neoclassical trait). If all property is private, states as we know them cannot exist; hence borders cannot exist; hence they are irrelevant. As this is not the kind of truth we are looking for, condition 3 could do with a reformulation as well. If Belgium had property, break-up also implies that some kind of deal about the distribution of Belgian state property between Flanders and Wallonia should be struck. By definition, the distribution of property rights influences the distribution of the pie. Does it also influence the size of the pie? Here we meet another and better known irrelevance proposition: Coase's (1960). His proposition is that the distribution of property rights is irrelevant for the efficiency of economic outcomes, as long as 1 there is a clear distribution of property rights, 2 there is freedom of contract, and 3 transaction costs are zero. The implication of Coase's proposition for Nordhaus *et al.*'s is that if transaction costs are zero and if Flanders and Wallonia can quickly agree on a new and clear distribution of Belgian property and if freedom of contract is granted, then there would be no effect on the size of the pie.

The state not only possesses goods, it also provides goods. A necessary condition for a border irrelevance proposition to hold is that there be no economies of scale in the provision of public goods. Robinson, in his aforementioned book (Robinson 1960: 225), has argued that such scale effects do exist. Concerning the costs of administration, he wrote that 'the number of members of a central legislature [is] dictated to a greater extent by the number of persons that can conveniently and efficiently take part in a debate'. Assuming defence costs to be related to the length of the border, 'as every schoolboy knows, if one doubles the dimensions of a given figure – a circle, a rectangle, or any figure that is similar in the two cases – the circumference is doubled while the area is quadrupled' (Robinson 1960: 235). These arguments seem little relevant to real world problems. We assume that the costs of ruling and defending Belgium are equal to the costs of ruling and defending Flanders and Wallonia.

4 Free trade between Flanders and Wallonia should be allowed. Here it is assumed implicitly that goods could move freely within Belgium. Again, such an assumption is plausible enough for a twentieth century state, but it is certainly not a universal truth. France before 1789 was an example of a state that was not a free trade area; originally the slogan *laissez faire, laissez passer* was an appeal to abandon internal French tariffs. But if we assume that goods can move freely within states, then there should be a free trade agreement between Flanders and Wallonia. However, this is not enough. Flanders and Wallonia should also copy Belgian trade policy with respect to third states, in this case Holland. In other words, a free trade agreement is not enough; what is needed is a Customs Union, and this Customs Union should take over the Belgian arrangements for the break-up not to have economic effects.

5 Belgian government income redistribution should be absent. Underlying this condition is the assumption that there is no redistribution between states, so that Flanders and Wallonia cannot decide to copy the Belgian redistribution policy. The assumption that there is no redistribution between states is unrealistic (think of development aid). However, it is true that redistribution between states is of a nature and size that is entirely different from redistribution within states. Therefore the condition that (Belgian) government income redistribution should be absent is basically correct.

For the 'Border Irrelevance Proposition' to be any good, the necessary conditions taken together should be a sufficient condition for the proposition to hold. Unfortunately this is certainly not so. For example, one obvious absentee condition is factor mobility. Borders matter when they obstruct the free mobility of labour and capital, even though to some extent free trade can be a substitute for free factor mobility. Hence, in spite of our reformulations, the 'Border Irrelevance Proposition' is still pretty lousy. The justification for its discussion here is that it has given us at least some idea of where to look for the economic effects of political break-up. Below we introduce two economic effects of political break-up that do not fit very well in the neoclassical framework.

6 A state chooses its economic system. The economic performance of capitalist and communist economies has been widely divergent over the last decades. So for Belgian break-up not to

have economic effects, Flanders and Wallonia should copy the Belgian economic system. Similarly, if Belgium was in a transition from one economic system to another, then Flanders and Wallonia should copy the Belgian transition strategy if the proposition is to hold.

7 Belgium, Wallonia and Flanders should have similar 'standards and regulations'. The state decides on many subjects that are indirectly relevant to economics. The decision on which side of the road to drive, how narrow the railway gauge should be, what language should be spoken, what script should be used, and even what time it is (see below) is to a large extent taken by the state (Kindleberger 1983). If preferences differ in this respect, new barriers to trade could arise from political break-up.

To summarise, the effects of Belgian break-up on the size of the pie and its distribution are more pronounced:

1 the more the monetary regimes of Flanders and Wallonia differ;
2 the more concentration in Wallonian and Flemish industries exists *if* there is no free trade between Flanders and Wallonia (if free trade is allowed, concentration is irrelevant);
3 the more difficulty Flanders and Wallonia have in agreeing upon a distribution of Belgian state property rights;
4 the higher trade and factor barriers between the two are, and the more Flemish, Wallonian and Belgian external trade policies differ;
5 the more the Belgian government redistributed before break-up;
6 the more transition strategies differ *if* preferences with respect to the economic system are on the move;
7 the more the standards and regulations introduced by the new states differ.

THE SIZE OF THE PIE AND ITS DISTRIBUTION

Once we are convinced that break-up is likely to have at least some economic effects, the next question is: *what* effects? Does the pie grow or shrink? And can we predict who can expect to obtain a larger part of it? Bolton and Roland (1995: 2) have proposed an answer that I will call, in analogy to Nordhaus *et al.*'s 'Border Irrelevance Proposition', a 'Border Losses Proposition'. This is how they formulate it:

From an economic efficiency point of view it is never desirable for a nation to separate into several independent parts. A unified nation is always more efficient since free trade among the regions is guaranteed, since duplication costs in defense and law enforcement are avoided, and since local public goods provision such as transportation and communication networks or common standards can be coordinated. Furthermore, any benefits of decentralization that might be obtained in a world with several nations can always be achieved within a unified nation by replicating the administrative structure of the world with several nations. Thus, if the most efficient economic arrangement was always prevailing, we would see only one nation with a suitable degree of decentralization of authority among regions.

(Bolton and Roland 1995: 2)

This paragraph deserves some careful analysis. It comes up with three of the issues that we discussed in the previous section: 3 economies of scale in the provision of public goods, 4 free trade, and 7 standards and regulations. All other issues are dealt with by the claim that all the potential advantages of having many states can also be obtained within a single state. But that claim is false once one defines a state as a free trade area, as Bolton and Roland do (or a monetary area – but the issue of money is not discussed by Bolton and Roland). Once a state is defined as a free trade area, a part of that state can no longer raise a tariff on goods from neighbouring parts of the same state. Similarly, once a state is defined as a monetary union, a part of the state can no longer introduce its own currency. However, as we shall make clear below, standard economic analysis on trade areas (Viner's Customs Union analysis) and monetary areas (Mundell's Optimum Currency Area analysis) make clear that there are costs and benefits to being a member of a trade area or a monetary area. Break-up allows the parts to make a cost–benefit analysis and then decide whether they want to stay in the trade or monetary area or not. But as long as the parts are united in a single state, this is not an option. Therefore, if a state is defined as a free trade area or as a monetary union, then it is no longer true that all the potential benefits of 'decentralisation' can also be obtained without leaving the state. There may be economic advantages to break-up, not only for the parts, but also for the whole.

Let us now return to conditions 1–7. We classify an effect as bearing on the size of the pie if it affects the wealth of Flanders and Wallonia similarly (both gain or both lose). If the effect is of a zero-sum-game character, the effect is on the pie's distribution.

1 Participation in a Monetary Union involves costs and benefits for the potential partners (see Chapter 6). The benefits, the reduction of risks and transaction costs can be related to the intensity of mutual trade. If trade links between Wallonia and Flanders are strong, there are important advantages to be gained from a common currency. Costs arise because the participants must forgo monetary autonomy. This is a serious disadvantage if countries have different preferences with respect to inflation, or if the exchange rate is an important tool of economic policy. The importance of the exchange rate as a policy instrument depends in turn on the availability of alternatives, such as labour mobility or fiscal redistribution between Flanders and Wallonia.

However, monetary autonomy is not necessarily an asset. If the ability to control inflation depends on the credibility of the central bank's commitment to do so, then countries can benefit from a loss of monetary autonomy if they opt for a common currency with partners that have a good reputation for fighting inflation. Rules can be better than discretion.

2 If concentration ratios in industries are high and free trade between Flanders and Wallonia is not allowed, the size of the pie decreases.

3 The distribution of state property rights does not influence the size of the pie as long as it proceeds quickly and clearly (assuming transaction costs are zero and there is freedom of contract). If not, the pie shrinks.

4 The notion that world wealth is maximised under world free trade is part of our creed. If there are no trade barriers between Belgium and Holland, then the pie is maximised if there are no trade barriers between Flanders and Wallonia either. But if there is a tariff between Holland and Belgium, then the creation of a tariff between Wallonia and Flanders can increase the size of the pie.

Suppose that Belgium had no internal tariffs, but did levy tariffs on Dutch goods. Possibly Wallonians bought goods in Flanders that they could have obtained cheaper in Holland if it were not for the tariff. Now Belgium breaks up, and the Wallonians decide to have the same tariff policy *vis-à-vis* both Flanders and Holland. The Wallonians now buy their goods and services in Holland, which increases Wallonian wealth. This is Viner's 'trade diversion' effect (Viner 1950: 44). The reduction in trade diversion increases the size of the pie.

On the other hand, the introduction of tariffs between Flanders and Wallonia could lead the Wallonians to produce goods and services that they used to buy in Flanders. This is the trade creation effect, or more exactly the opposite of it (which is obviously something very different from trade diversion). This causes the pie to decrease. Hence, the overall effects of tariff introduction between Wallonia and Flanders is dependent on the relative sizes of trade de-diversion and trade de-creation. The size of the pie increases if trade de-diversion is bigger than trade de-creation.

It is hard to imagine how a reduction in factor mobility between Wallonia and Flanders would increase the pie. For Common Markets, there is no 'theory of the second best' argument that is analogous to the Customs Union argument. Barriers to factor mobility between Flanders and Wallonia are likely to decrease the size of the pie, as generally speaking labour and capital should be employed where marginal returns are highest, and any obstruction to this is pie reducing. But for the constituent parts, there can very well be benefits from obstacles to factor mobility. Parts that suffer from brain drain or capital flight could benefit from the creation of barriers. The distribution of the pie can change.

If the creation of a border is not followed up by the creation of a Common Market, a reorientation in external economic relations is likely to take place. In the present case, the introduction of the same barriers between Flanders and Wallonia as the ones that already existed between Belgium and Holland makes Holland a relatively more attractive economic partner. The reorientation of economic activity is costly, however, because exchange of goods, labour and capital implies transport, and transport implies infrastructure. Obvious examples are railways, telecommunication networks, electricity grids, and oil pipelines. Capital has been invested in infrastructure that facilitated exchange with other parts of the country. In the new situation, exchange with new partners could require a huge initial capital outlay, and the old infrastructure rusts out. The size of the pie diminishes.

5 The break-up of states does not change the combined wealth of the parts involved because of the role of the state as a redistributor, but it increases the wealth of some regions and reduces that of others.

6 We assume that the transition from a centrally planned economy to a market economy necessarily contains three elements: stabilisation, liberalisation and privatisation. Stabilisation is defined here to concern the price level only. In our view, inflation is a monetary phenomenon. We have already dealt with this aspect of political break-up when we discussed the monetary aspects; therefore this aspect of transition can be found in [1c] in Table 2.1.

As with stabilisation, in principle it should be considered an advantage to have the opportunity to design liberalisation and privatisation strategies that take into account the specific problems of the region. However, in these respects as well, rules can be better than discretion, as we shall make clear presently (in the next section under [6a] and [6b]).

7 Introducing barriers to trade by introducing different standards and regulations reduces welfare. In some cases, however, a switch is made from a standard that was used by the old partners to a standard used by prospective new partners. If this helps to reduce barriers to trade with the new partners, a new standard can also be welfare improving.

Table 2.1 Economic effects of political break-up

Effects:	Size	Distribution
1a Monetary: transaction costs	−	
1b Monetary: exchange rate adjustment	+	
1c Monetary: inflation = transition: stabilisation	+/−	
2 Competition	0/−	
3 Property rights	0/−	Δ
4a Trade	+/−	
4b Labour and capital	0/−	Δ
4c Infrastructure	0/−	
5 Income redistribution		Δ
6a Transition: liberalisation	+/−	
6b Transition: privatisation	+/−	
7 Standards and regulations	+/−	

Δ means change.

Table 2.1 summarises the potential effects of break-up that we have discussed thus far. We show how these effects work out in the case of the Soviet Union in the next section.

SOVIET BREAK-UP

Using our checklist, let us see what the economic effects of Soviet break-up are.

1a *Transaction costs* All Newly Independent States (NIS) lose because the break-up of the rouble zone implies that transactions with other NIS entail higher costs than before. The high level of integration between the NIS that existed under the *ancien régime* (van Selm and Wagener 1993; see Chapter 4) suggests that increases in transaction costs can be serious. But an assessment of future external economic relations of NIS based on a gravity model (van Selm 1995b; see Chapter 5 and also van Selm 1995a, c) indicates that trade with third countries can be expected to become more important than intra-NIS trade. If this expectation materialises, the increase in transaction costs would be less severe.

1b *Exchange rate adjustment* All NIS that have left the rouble zone gain because they have an extra instrument of economic policy. This is an important gain, because alternative mechanisms for adjustment to an asymmetric shock, such as fiscal redistribution or labour mobility, are absent. Yet, adjustment is likely to be necessary, given the fact that the economic structure of the NIS economies is very different. For example, the production of oil and gas is heavily concentrated in Russia. These products' export to world markets can be realised at short notice. In turn, this would lead to an increased demand for roubles, and hence to a rouble exchange rate that renders the products of other republics on world markets too expensive. By having a separate currency, the possibility to devalue *vis-à-vis* the rouble is created.

1c *Inflation–stabilisation* The break-up of the rouble zone enables the NIS to do better or worse than Russia in stabilisation. The three Baltic republics seized this opportunity in 1993. Within the Commonwealth of Independent States (CIS), Russia's inflation was lowest. The effect of the break-up of the rouble zone on Russian inflation was positive (i.e. rouble inflation reducing), because it solved the free rider problem that existed with a number of independent fiscal authorities joining a single currency.

2   *Competition* As trade between the republics is not free at present and as the degree of monopolisation of the Soviet economy was high, all republics presently suffer from the negative consequences of monopolies. To give an impression of the rate of concentration, in 1991 a single plant in Belarus (the world's largest) produced 90 per cent of the Soviet Union's polyester and a single plant in Russia (the 'Togliatti Volga Automobile Works Named After the 50th Anniversary of the Soviet Union') produced 58 per cent of the Union's automobiles (Krugman and Obstfeld 1994: 713).

3   *Property rights* The distribution of Soviet property among the successor states has proceeded fairly smoothly. The territorial principle has rigidly been applied. For example, Russia has never contested the fact that Baikonur, the Soviet space centre that happened to be located in Kazakhstan, is now Kazakh property. Today Russia pays rent for the use of it. Enterprises that used to be under All-Union control were similarly distributed according to their location. The distribution of mobile assets has been fairly efficient as well. For example, for the Soviet merchant fleet, the following distribution is reported: Russia 56 per cent, Ukraine 26 per cent, Latvia 5.6 per cent, Estonia 3.2 per cent, Lithuania 1.9 per cent, Georgia 2.8 per cent, Azerbaidzjan 3.1 per cent (Clement 1993: 134). With respect to Soviet foreign liabilities, Russia has taken responsibility for all, in return for the inheritance of former Soviet foreign assets. The Black Sea Fleet is the exception to the rule.

4a   *Trade* The above-mentioned gravity analysis result indicates that trade with non-NIS partners is likely to be more important than intra-NIS trade if there is no institutional bias in favour of a particular group of trade partners. This implies that the risk of trade diversion is serious if a Customs Union between the NIS is maintained. Therefore the NIS gain by the break-up of the former Soviet Customs Union.

Historical evidence supports this conclusion. In the case of Central Asia,

> before the arrival of the Russians, Bukhara's excellent location made it an important link between India and Europe. By 1894, Russia imposed a Customs Union upon

Bukhara . . . which involved the closing of the Bukharan-
Afghan frontier and the consequent blocking of the direct
entry of all Indian goods. From this time on there was no
problem of competition for Russian goods, which increased in quantity in the Central Asian market

(Allworth 1989: 322)

The Baltic economies experienced a similar fate after conquest.
In the *interbellum*, they were able to enter into world markets
with fair success (Arkadie and Karlsson 1991: 5), whereas after
1945 trade with the non-Soviet world was virtually impossible.
Therefore, the fact that exchange was extensive in Soviet days
does not prove that Russia was a natural partner for either the
Baltic States or Central Asia; existing exchange may well have
been of a trade-diverting character.

4b *Labour and capital* Ethnic rather than economic factors determine the pattern of intra-NIS migration. Labour is returning to
its 'home' republic on a large scale. This causes, for example,
severe economic trouble in Central Asia, because its industries
were mainly staffed by Russian personnel. More generally, all
republics lose because labour allocation is not determined by its
marginal product.

Capital flows among the Soviet republics were unrequited
and can therefore be dealt with as government redistribution
(see (5)).

4c *Infrastructure* The existing infrastructure facilitates exchange
among the NIS, not exchange with non-NIS states. The common Soviet railway gauge, a few centimetres wider than the
European gauge, can serve as an example here. For the Baltic
republics, this inheritance of Soviet rule implies that the time
spent on a railway trip to Moscow is much shorter than that to
Warsaw, even though the latter is closer in distance. In the
Communist era, these republics were almost completely Moscow oriented in their foreign economic exchange, so that this
made at least some economic sense. Today, Western Europe is
likely to become a much more important economic partner,
and infrastructural investments will be required to link the
Baltic economies to those of Western Europe. Oil and gas
pipelines are another example. Turkmenistan continues to
pump gas to Ukraine, notwithstanding the fact that Ukraine
is a very bad debtor. But unfortunately for the Turkmens, this

is the country to which the Turkmen gas pipes lead. Ukraine used to buy 40 per cent of Turkmen production (Vanous 1994: 3). Constructing a new pipeline is expensive and takes time.

5 *Government income redistribution* Redistribution flows among the fifteen republics were very significant in the former Soviet Union (van Selm and Dölle 1993; see Chapter 8). Less developed republics like Kirgizstan and Uzbekistan annually received more than 10 per cent of their GNPs in donations from other republics; for a developed republic like Belarus a net contribution of 15–20 per cent of GNP to the rest of the Union was quite normal.

These figures change when 'world market' prices instead of internal Soviet prices are used in calculations. If this is done, Russia emerges from the analysis as the overimportant subsidiser of all other Soviet republics (except Turkmenistan). If this is correct, the implication is that Russia has much to gain from the end of redistribution, whereas all other republics have much to lose.

6a *Liberalisation* Liberalisation strategies differ among the republics. In Russia, the liberalisation of the economy has been fairly comprehensive, though far from complete. The federal government still controls the price of gas, domestic electricity, water, telephone calls and intercity transportation. Local authorities directly control municipal transport prices and public housing rents. They also have the right to control consumer prices, but the cost of such price controls must be borne by the local budget (Centre for Economic Reforms 1993: 28). Conversely, in Ukraine,

> although a range of prices was freed from formal administrative controls in 1992, Ukraine remained to an important extent a shortage economy. Inability to obtain goods at posted prices in the state distribution network remained a notable constraint on consumption. Similarly, the output of many enterprises was restrained by lack of inputs rather than by insufficient demand for their products at the going prices. Parallel markets remained in existence for most consumer and many industrial goods. Official estimates suggest that regulated prices applied to 57 percent of wholesale turnover and 67 percent of retail turnover. 'Free'

prices were estimated to apply to 26 percent of wholesale turnover and to 21 percent of retail turnover.

(IMF 1993: 54)

As with stabilisation, Moscow rules with respect to liberalisation would have been better than Kiev discretion for Ukraine.

Price liberalisation in the Baltic republics was more comprehensive than in Russia; in Central Asia it was less. All three Baltic republics have freed virtually all prices (Schroeder 1994: 2). In Uzbekistan, Turkmenistan and Tadzjikistan, price controls and state orders are presently used more extensively than in Russia (Schroeder 1994: 9). Kazakhstan and Kirgizstan have done better in this respect (Schroeder 1994: 8).

6b *Privatisation.* The privatisation tale is similar to that of stabilisation and liberalisation. In Russia, the voucher privatisation programme has progressed more rapidly than privatisation programmes elsewhere in the CIS. By the end of 1993, a total of 89,000 Russian enterprises had been privatised (Vanous 1994: 26). Conversely, in Ukraine at the end of 1992 the government issued a decree listing the types of enterprise *not* subject to privatisation. All other enterprises are available for sale once someone expresses an interest in them (IMF 1993: 56). As few people have done so, very little progress has been made.

Progress has been made in the Baltic republics (Schroeder 1994: 3), whereas in Central Asia less has been achieved. Kazakhstan and Kirgizstan are moving somewhat more slowly with respect to privatisation than Russia (Schroeder 1994: 8); in Uzbekistan, Turkmenistan and Tadzjikistan, 'although the three states have adopted programs for the privatisation of state property, they intend that the process apply to small enterprises, with the large ones substantially if not entirely remaining in the hands of the state, (Schroeder 1994: 9).

7 *Standards and regulations* To some extent, having been a single country is equivalent to being a single country, because of path dependencies. Having been a single and united country implies that common standards and regulations have existed for a certain period of time. After break-up, the newly formed states could in principle decide to introduce different standards and regulations. However, often it is expensive to change a standard once it exists. Therefore newly formed states continue to have

23

similar standards and regulations, even though they are no longer a single country. For example, it is not to be expected that some NIS will start driving on the left side of the road. Similarly, changing the railway gauge is very expensive. It is less clear that no NIS shall attempt this, however, because of the narrower gauge in the rest of Europe. The three Baltic republics had narrow gauges before conquest in 1940 and may try to reswitch.

Some standards have been changed already. In an attempt to facilitate interaction with the non-NIS part of the world, Uzbekistan has switched to using Latin script instead of Cyrillic. Kiev moved from Moscow time (GMT +3) to Helsinki–Bucharest time (GMT +2). To express its adhesion to Moscow, Crimea subsequently reswitched to Moscow time.

Table 2.2 summarises the results that we have obtained. We distinguish among four macro-regions: Russia, Ukraine, the Baltic republics and Central Asia.

Two conclusions can be drawn from this evidence. First, the negative signs dominate the positive ones. Even though we have said nothing about the size of these effects, we could conjecture that the net effect of break-up is negative. Second, the signs are in the same direction for all republics, except for the effects related to transition and redistribution. From the table, we could derive the hypothesis that the economic performance of Russia and the Baltic

Table 2.2 Economic effects of Soviet break-up

Effects	Russia	Ukraine	Baltics	Central Asia	Sum
Transaction costs	−	−	−	−	−
Exchange rate adjustment	+	+	+	+	+
Inflation–stabilisation	+	−	+	−	+/−
Competition	−	−	−	−	−
Property rights	−	−	−	−	−
Trade	+	+	+	+	+
Factors	−	−	−	−	−
Infrastructure	−	−	−	−	−
Redistribution	+	−	−	−	0
Transition: liberalisation	+	−	+	−	+/−
Transition: privatisation	+	−	+	−	+/−
Standards and regulations	0	0	0	0	0

Table 2.3 Post-Soviet economic performance

	GNP growth over previous year					
	1990	1991	1992	1993	1994	1995*
Russia	−4	−13	−19	−12	−15	−3
Ukraine	−3	−12	−17	−17	−23	−5
Belarus	−3	−1	−10	−12	−22	−10
Uzbekistan	2	−1	−11	−2	−3	−4
Kazakhstan	0	−13	−13	−12	−25	−12
Georgia	−12	−14	−40	−39	−35	−5
Azerbaidzjan	−12	−1	−23	−23	−22	−15
Lithuania	−5	−13	−38	−24	2	5
Moldova	−2	−12	−29	−9	−22	−5
Latvia	3	−8	−35	−15	2	1
Kirgizstan	3	−5	−25	−16	−27	−5
Tadzjikistan	−2	−7	−29	−11	−21	−12
Armenia	−7	−11	−52	−15	5	5
Turkmenistan	2	−5	−5	−10	−20	−5
Estonia	−8	−11	−14	−7	6	6

Source: EBRD (1995: 185)   * = projection

republics should improve relative to that of Ukraine and Central Asia. In the data on the republics' GNP since the break-up of the USSR presented in Table 2.3, we can find some support for this conclusion.

CONCLUSION

This chapter has shown that the economic effects of political break-up are manifold. The 'Border Irrelevance Proposition' is a useful logical construction, but along with Nordhaus et al. we would argue that it is clearly wrong in reality. Starting from this proposition we developed a checklist of potential economic effects of political break-up, and we applied it to the Soviet Union in the second part of the chapter. Assessing a net economic gain or loss per former Soviet republic may well be impossible. Also it is a little early to determine what the economic effects of political break-up are. It will be possible to make a better judgement after, say, twenty years of independence. Any conclusion is therefore necessarily provisional.

In our analysis of the economic effects of break-up we found more negative than positive effects. A tentative conclusion could be that there are more losses than gains. It is almost certain, for example, that trade patterns will be different after break-up, and hence that the infrastructure must be adapted, which is costly. Property rights distribution is difficult and likely to lead to an interim period of indeterminate property rights, which is bad for economic performance. Reduction of competition if there is no free trade is welfare reducing as well. We guess that these effects are more important than the potential advantages, such as the reduction in trade diversion and the gain of the exchange rate as an instrument of economic policy.

Two aspects bear on the relative performances of the NIS: redistribution and transition. On account of these two variables, we expect Russia and the Baltics to do better than Ukraine and Central Asia in the near future. However, the economic performance of the Newly Independent States is also influenced by factors that are not related to break-up. Obvious factors are raw material and human resource endowments, as well as economic structure and the level of development. Differences among the republics in these respects are discussed in the next chapter.

3

THE SOVIET UNION, 1922–91

Союз Нерушимый Республик Свободных
Сплотила Навеки Великая Русь
Да Здраствует Созданный Волей Народов
Единый Могучий Советский Союз

An Eternal Union of Free Republics
Rallied round Russia the Great.
Praise the Mighty Work of the People's Will:
The One and Only Soviet Union!
(Soviet National Anthem, lines 1–4,
Author's translation)

THE RISE AND FALL OF THE UNION

The first four lines of the Soviet National Anthem contain at least
three errors. First, with the benefit of hindsight, we can now say
that the Soviet Union was not eternal. Instead, it lasted exactly
sixty-nine years minus four days. The Union Treaty was signed on
the stage of Moscow's Bolshoi Theatre on 30 December 1922.
Gorbachev formally dissolved the Union on 26 December 1991.

Second, the Union was not created by the People's will, but by
Stalin. As the Commissar of Nationalities, he drew up a draft
concerning the relations between Russia and the other republics.
It stressed the voluntariness of the Union in letter, but implied
complete subordination to Moscow in practice. Leaders in favour of
a more equal distribution of power among the republics were either
dying (Lenin) or helped by Stalin in doing so. In the spring of 1922,
a commission headed by Michael Frunze worked out a proposal on
the relations between Russia and the Ukraine that expressed equality in the relations between the two, both in letter and in spirit.

Frunze's ideas were unsuccessful and he paid a high price for them. On 30 October 1925, against his own will but obeying party discipline, Frunze submitted himself to a medical operation. This was Stalin's first medical murder (Svoboda 1992: 781).

The republics were not 'free' either to join or to leave (error number three), even though the original Union Treaty included as its final article, article 26, a right of secession by each union republic from the Union. This constitutional 'right to secede' has been repeated in every successive USSR Constitution (1924, art.4; 1936, art.17; 1977, art.72; see Henderson 1991: 47). However, before perestroika, this was a dead letter.

The most revealing aspect of the songlines that were copied above is the explicit reference to 'Russia the Great'. In many respects the Soviet Union was merely a continuation of the Tsarist empire. Both tended to expand (witness the annexation of Transcaucasia and Central Asia in the nineteenth century, and of the Baltic republics and Moldova in the twentieth) and both were dominated by Russians in power more than in numbers. The imperial Russian census of 1897 counted only 44.3 per cent of the total population as Russians; in 1926 the Soviet Union counted 52.6 per cent (Pearson 1991: 21). The explanation of this difference lies mainly in the loss of western territories (Poland) in the period of the transition from the Tsarist to the Soviet state. The fact that Russia itself saw the Soviet Union as a kind of Russian empire is illustrated by the fact that Russia was the only republic that did not see fit to issue a declaration of independence in 1990–1 (see Table 3.1).

Equally illuminating is the fact that when in 1945 the Soviet Union demanded a seat for each of the republics in the United Nations General Assembly and obtained three seats as a compromise, Russia did not obtain one. Instead, the two other Slav republics, Ukraine and Belarus, second and third in the Soviet family hierarchy, were allocated one each. The third seat was for the Union. The Slavic republics and especially Russia thus had a dominant position in the Union. However, non-Slav individuals did have a chance to move up on the Soviet ladder, as the example of Stalin (a Georgian) proves.

Formally at least, the Soviet Union was a Union of fifteen Soviet Socialist Republics (SSRs) from 1955 to 1990. Each of these SSRs was meant to represent one of the countries' biggest ethnic groups, and each was nominally identified with one. Originally the Union had only four SSRs: the RSFSR (Russian Soviet Federal Socialist

Table 3.1 The Union's break-up

	Sovereignty	Independence
Russia	12 June 1990 (5)	–
Ukraine	16 July 1990 (8)	19 August 1991 (5)
Belarus	27 July 1990 (10)	26 August 1991 (6)
Kazakhstan	25 October 1990 (14)	16 December 1991 (14)
Uzbekistan	20 June 1990 (6)	31 August 1991 (9)
Georgia	20 June 1990 (7)	9 April 1991 (4)
Azerbaidzjan	23 September 1989 (4)	30 August 1991 (8)
Lithuania	28 May 1989 (2)	11 March 1990 (1)
Moldova	26 July 1990 (9)	27 August 1991 (7)
Latvia	28 July 1989 (3)	4 May 1990 (3)
Kirgizstan	27 October 1990 (15)	31 August 1991 (10)
Tadzjikistan	24 August 1990 (13)	9 September 1991 (11)
Armenia	23 August 1990 (12)	23 September 1991 (12)
Turkmenistan	22 August 1990 (11)	27 October 1991 (13)
Estonia	16 November 1988 (1)	30 March 1990 (2)

Sources: CEC (1993); van den Berg (1991: 230); and RFE/RL Report (1994). This is the order in Soviet republics as it was found in official postwar Soviet publications. It is based on the size of the population in 1940 and was not changed when, for example, Kazakhstan and Uzbekistan overtook Belarus in population size. We shall stick to this format throughout this volume. Less conservative is our spelling of the republics: we shall not refer to Moldavia, Kirgizia, Turkmenia, Byelorussia, or RSFSR

Republic), the TSFSR (Transcaucasian etc.), and the Ukrainian and Belarussian SSRs. At that time the Russian Federation included Central Asia. The Central Asian republics acquired the status of Union republics in 1924 (Turkmenistan), 1925 (Uzbekistan), 1929 (Tadzjikistan) and 1936 (Kirgizstan and Kazakhstan). Also in 1936 the Transcaucasian SFSR was split into Azerbaidzjan, Armenia and Georgia. The Moldovan and the Baltic (Lithuanian, Latvian, Estonian) SSRs were set up following the conquest of these territories in 1940, and they took on a more definitive shape upon the *reconquista* in 1944–5. The number of SSRs was at its peak (sixteen) from 1945 to 1955. A Karelo-Finnish SSR covered the territory that the Soviet Union took from Finland in 1940. In 1955, a part of the territory taken in 1940 was returned to Finland, and the rest of the Karelo-Finnish Union Republic was integrated in the Russian Federation as the Karelian Autonomous Republic (Karelian ASSR). The 1955 situation remained unchanged until 1990–1, when all fifteen Union republics were accepted as independent states by the international community.

The ethnic principle also played a role on the lower levels of territorial–administrative organisation. Second after the SSRs were the ASSRs, the 'Autonomous' republics. Some of these have state ambitions today. On 15 February 1994, Tatarstan, formerly an ASSR within Russia, and Russia signed a treaty describing Tatarstan as 'a state united to Russia'. Abkhazia, formerly an ASSR within Georgia, fought its way out. And Chechnya, half of what was the Chechen–Ingush Autonomous Republic within Russia in Soviet times, declared itself to be an independent state in 1991. Chechen independence was, however, crushed when Russian forces attacked its capital Grozny in December 1994 and conquered the town, or what was left of it, in early 1995. None of these ex-ASSRs has yet been recognised by the international community as an independent state.

On a still lower level, eight Autonomous Oblasts and ten Autonomous Okrugs existed – for example, Nagorno Karabakh Autonomous Oblast in Azerbaidzjan, and the Jewish Autonomous Oblast in Eastern Siberia. These areas were also situated on the territory of an SSR. Areas of SSRs that were not part of any of the 'national' areas were subdivided into oblasts or krais. To complicate matters further, however, there were also national areas that were not directly part of an SSR, but part of an okrug or krai. None of these territorial–administrative arrangements was very relevant in Soviet times. As we stressed before, the Soviet Union was a highly centralised state in all but letter. The behaviour of Soviet leaders was in accordance with the irrelevance of intra-USSR borders. For example, in 1954 Khrushchev took the Crimea from Russia and gave it as a present to the Ukraine. With the break-up of the Soviet Union, however, the frontiers between the Union republics have all of a sudden become highly significant. The Khrushchev gift could well turn out to have major negative effects.

The Baltic republics were the first to declare themselves sovereign, meaning that their laws were more important than those of the Union. Subsequently more republics issued a similar declaration, and negotiations over a new Union Treaty started. In March 1991, a draft was signed by the three Slavic and the five Central Asian republics. In these republics plus Azerbaidzjan, a Referendum for the Continuation of the Union was held on 17 March 1991. At that time, many were still favouring the Union. In Ukraine, for example, 70 per cent voted in favour of the Union.

Support for the Union was also quite high in Central Asia. The Draft Union Treaty that was supposed to be signed on 20 August 1991 allowed Georgia, Armenia, Moldova, Estonia, Latvia and Lithuania to secede, and increased the rights of the remaining nine republics in relation to the centre. On the 19th, Yanayev *cum suis* undertook a final attempt to save the old Union, but instead his abortive coup destroyed both the old and the new. On 26 December 1991, the Union was formally dissolved.

On 21 December 1991, eleven of the fifteen republics signed an agreement in Alma-Ata (now Almaty), establishing the Commonwealth of Independent States (CIS, in Russian Sodruzhestvo Nezavissimykh Gosydarstv, SNG). The three Baltic republics were not interested, and neither was Georgia at first. However, civil war in the latter republic led President Shevardnadze to opt for CIS membership in October 1993, in an attempt to lure the Red Army into the battle. Azerbaidzjan also had a short spell outside the CIS. As in the case of Georgia, however, military disaster (in the war with Armenia) drove it back to Russia.

In March 1996, the Russian State Duma passed resolutions that affirmed the 'legal force' of the referendum that was held on 17 March 1991 and rejected the December 1991 accords that formed the CIS and abrogated the 1922 treaty forming the USSR. The Duma thus asserted that the USSR legally continues to exist. However, these resolutions were met with sharp criticism by the Russian President and by the leaders of the other successor states, with the exception of Belarussian president Lukashenka. It will take more than Russian Duma resolutions to revive the USSR.

THE REPUBLICS' INPUTS: LAND, LABOUR, CAPITAL

A casual look at a map of the former Soviet Union (FSU) makes clear that the size of the republics' territories is widely divergent. Even Ukraine, about the size of France, looks tiny when compared to Russia. For the economist, the main trouble with the size of the Russian Federation relative to the rest of the Union is encountered when applying gravity analysis, and we shall return to this problem later on. Table 3.2 presents the shares of the republics in union territory (22,277,000 square kilometres) as well as the dominant form of this territory.

Economists view land as a factor of production. The FSU land

Table 3.2 The republics' land

	Percentage of Union total	Main form of landscape
Russian Federation	76.6	Tayga
Ukraine	2.7	Steppe
Belarus	0.9	Forest
Uzbekistan	2.0	Desert (Kizilkum)
Kazakhstan	12.2	Steppe
Georgia	0.3	Mountains (Big Caucasus)
Azerbaidzjan	0.4	Steppe
Lithuania	0.3	Forest
Moldova	0.2	Steppe
Latvia	0.3	Forest
Kirgizstan	0.9	Mountains (Tien Shan)
Tadzjikistan	0.6	Mountains (Pamir)
Armenia	0.1	Mountains (Small Caucasus)
Turkmenistan	2.2	Desert (Karakum)
Estonia	0.2	Forest

Sources: World Bank (1992: 4–5) for territories; landscapes collected from data in Mellor (1988) and Noble and King (1991). The 'main form of landscape' covers at least 50 per cent of the area of the republic in question. The 'Tayga' is a coniferous forest, typical of Russia: 'This is a gloomy, silent, forbidding forest; to venture into them, it is said, is to know the meaning of fear' (Mellor 1988: 11). The other terms are self-evident

certainly has a huge economic potential, with huge energy resources in Russia and Central Asia (oil, gas, and water power), as well as rich mineral endowments, including gold (mainly in Russia) plus diamonds; and large areas of arable land in Russia, the Ukraine and Kazakhstan. To exploit such riches, a second factor of production is indispensable: people.

As the data in Tables 3.2 and 3.3 show, land and labour are heterogeneous factors of production, and this is especially true for the former Soviet Union. An essential precondition for economic success is cooperation among people. This requires mutual understanding. The fourth column in Table 3.3 makes it clear that efforts to achieve this were not undertaken by the Russians. The Russian language was the lingua franca of the Union. With the collapse of the Union, all this is changing rapidly. The Russians are retreating from the peripheral republics, and especially from Central Asia. For example, in Tashkent the percentage of Uzbeks in the city's population has risen from 40 per cent in the early 1980s to 60 per cent today, on account of the Russian exodus. In a 1993 survey, 81 per

Table 3.3 The republics' peoples

	Percentage of Union total	Titular group (%)	Russians (%)	3rd group (%)
Russia	51.2	81.5	—	Tatars: 3.8
Ukraine	17.9	72.7	22.1	Jews: 0.9
Belarus	3.6	77.9	13.2	Poles: 4.1
Uzbekistan	7.1	71.4	8.3	Tadzjiks: 4.7
Kazakhstan	5.8	39.7	37.8	Germans: 5.8
Georgia	1.9	70.1	6.3	Armenians: 8.1
Azerbaidzjan	2.5	82.7	5.6	Armenians: 5.6
Lithuania	1.3	79.6	9.4	Poles: 7.0
Moldova	1.5	64.5	13.0	Ukrainians: 13.8
Latvia	0.9	52.0	34.0	Belarussians: 4.5
Kirgizstan	1.5	52.4	21.5	Uzbeks: 12.9
Tadzjikistan	1.9	62.3	7.6	Uzbeks: 23.5
Armenia	1.2	93.3	1.6	Azeris: 2.6
Turkmenistan	1.3	72.0	9.5	Uzbeks: 9.5
Estonia	0.6	61.5	30.3	Ukrainians: 3.1

Source: Compiled from Schwarz (1991). The Union total population was 290.1 million in 1988

cent of the Russian families living in Dushanbe, the capital of Tadzjikistan, indicated that they wanted to leave (Shamshur 1993: 2). Of the 918,000 Russians living in Kirgizstan in 1990, 170,000 had left by 1994. Such retreats of Slavic workers and professionals caused the virtual shutting down of some production lines in Central Asia (Shamshur 1993: 4). People are on the move in other parts of the FSU as well. Exchanges of refugees in the course of the Armenian–Azeri conflict totalled nearly 500,000 people (Shamshur 1993: 4).

A glance at the Soviet peoples' languages, scripts and beliefs (Table 3.4) shows just how different they were. The languages of the Armenians, Lithuanians, Latvians and Tadzjiks belong to the Indo-European group, as do the Slav and Romanic languages. The Turkic languages, Georgian and Estonian do not share this common root. After the Soviet conquest, the script was first changed from Arabic to Latin in all republics with a Turkic language, and later on Latin script was replaced by Cyrillic. Today, by reintroducing Latin script, Azerbaidzjan, Uzbekistan, Kirgizstan and Turkmenistan are moving back to an alphabet that they have used in only ten years of their histories. But a better interpretation would

Table 3.4 The peoples' tongues and beliefs

	Language group	Script group	Main religion
Russia	Slav	Cyrillic	Russian Orthodox
Ukraine	Slav	Cyrillic	Russian Orthodox
Belarus	Slav	Cyrillic	Russian Orthodox
Uzbekistan	Turkic	Cyrillic	Sunni
Kazakhstan	Turkic	Cyrillic	Sunni
Georgia	Georgian	Georgian	Georgian Orthodox
Azerbaidzjan	Turkic	Cyrillic	Shiite
Lithuania	Baltic	Latin	Catholic
Moldova	Romanic	Cyrillic	Orthodox
Latvia	Baltic	Latin	Lutheran
Kirgizstan	Turkic	Cyrillic	Sunni
Tadzjikistan	Iranian	Cyrillic	Sunni
Armenia	Armenian	Armenian	Armenian Orthodox
Turkmenistan	Turkic	Cyrillic	Sunni
Estonia	Finno-Ugrian	Latin	Lutheran

Sources: An old Soviet five rouble banknote for script, religions compiled from Noble and King (1991)

be to see it as a forward-looking move. Only in Tadzjikistan was it decided to return to Arabic script.

The republics also differ substantially in their third factor of production, i.e. the amount of capital invested and accumulated in them. Russia, Kazakhstan and the Baltic republics had more than proportional per capita capital formation, the other republics less. Investment allocation in the late 1980s reinforced this tendency; as an example, we have added the pattern of 1988 investment in Table 3.5.

THE REPUBLICS' OUTPUTS

The results in Table 3.6 show that differences in productivity (GNP per capita) were huge. To a large extent, these differences can be explained by differences in capital formation. The variation in production per capital invested is much lower than the variation in the production per capita. Kazakhstan stands out with a very low capital productivity. Ever since the start of the Virgin Lands Campaign in 1954, Kazakhstan has been a favourite location for Soviet investment (Rumer 1983: 215). In view of the low capital productivity, it is surprising that the republic received such large

Table 3.5 Capital investment in the republics, 1988

	1988 stock (% of Union)	1988 flow (% of Union)	Stock/capita (USSR = 100)	Flow/capita (USSR = 100)
Russia	61.4	63.4	119.0	122.8
Ukraine	15.6	13.5	86.2	74.6
Belarus	3.4	3.5	94.9	98.9
Uzbekistan	3.4	3.5	49.7	50.3
Kazakhstan	5.9	6.0	101.1	102.8
Georgia	1.4	1.4	74.1	74.0
Azerbaidzjan	1.5	1.6	69.7	71.8
Lithuania	1.4	1.5	110.1	112.8
Moldova	1.1	1.1	71.4	72.3
Latvia	1.1	0.9	114.0	95.1
Kirgizstan	0.8	0.7	50.2	47.9
Tadzjikistan	0.7	0.8	38.6	45.2
Armenia	0.8	0.7	64.5	59.0
Turkmenistan	0.9	0.9	75.5	77.0
Estonia	0.7	0.6	125.0	106.2

Source: Compiled from Goskomstat (1989b: 556) and from Burkett (1992: 166–8)

Table 3.6 The republics' aggregate output, 1988

	GNP/capita (USSR = 100)	GNP/capital stock (USSR = 100)
Russia	115.8	97.3
Ukraine	92.9	107.8
Belarus	116.6	122.8
Uzbekistan	51.1	102.9
Kazakhstan	71.5	70.8
Georgia	91.9	123.9
Azerbaidzjan	84.6	121.4
Lithuania	109.9	99.9
Moldova	85.1	119.1
Latvia	124.2	109.0
Kirgizstan	56.3	112.0
Tadzjikistan	45.8	118.0
Armenia	82.8	128.4
Turkmenistan	67.1	89.0
Estonia	121.6	97.2

Source: Compiled using Table 3.5, and from Burkett (1992: 166–8)

amounts of it: 'It is certainly not far-fetched to call Kazakhstan one of the sinks of the Soviet economy' (Wagener 1986: 157). The variation in GNP per capita implies that Breznjev was wrong when he declared, back in 1972, that 'the problem of equalizing the levels of development of the national republics has in the main been solved' (quoted in Holubnychy 1973: 25).

It is true, however, that attempts were made to reduce the gap in the development between poor and rich republics. Redistribution flows among Soviet republics were huge and important, and we shall return to them in Chapter 8. The main result of such an analysis is that attempts to reduce the gap were strong in the 1960s and 1970s, but declined in the 1980s.

The division of labour as it existed among the republics can to some extent be explained by geographic phenomena. Oil (Russia; some in Kazakhstan and Azerbaidzjan) and gas (Russia and Turkmenistan; some in Uzbekistan and the Ukraine) are produced where they are found; the production of steel takes place near the location of coal and iron ore (in the Ukraine and in Russia); cotton (Central Asia and Azerbaidzjan) requires a warm climate; relatively 'high-tech' products are naturally located in the more developed areas – hence the relatively high share in the production of TV sets and refrigerators in Lithuania and Belarus; the climate of the western republics is well suited for cattle breeding, whereas grain grows well on the Ukrainian and Kazakh Tsernozem parts of the steppe. Of the products listed in Table 3.7 one might criticise the authorities for the low share in cotton cloth production in Central Asia; however, in world history the production of clothes at the place of cotton growing has seldom proved profitable enough to be developed.

Hence, in a basic sense the division of labour as chosen by Moscow planners and as illustrated by Table 3.7 seems pretty rational and straightforward. But there are certainly some peculiarities as well. Owing to the central planners' unlimited faith in economies of scale, the production of many products was heavily concentrated in one or a few factories.

A description of the regional specialisation and a comprehensive test for the rationality of the pattern of specialisation in the Soviet Union was performed by Wagener (1973), and was repeated by Gillula (1979) with similar results. Wagener's results can be summarised as follows. Historical developments have resulted in a large amount of specialisation. That is, in the initial stage of industria-

Table 3.7 The republics' produce (as a percentage of Union total)

	Oil	Gas	Steel	Cotton	Cotton cloth
Russia	91.1	76.6	57.7	—	71.3
Ukraine	0.9	4.2	34.7	—	6.9
Belarus	0.3	0.04	0.7	—	1.7
Uzbekistan	0.4	5.2	0.6	61.0	5.6
Kazakhstan	4.1	0.9	4.2	3.7	1.8
Georgia	0.03	0.01	0.9	—	0.7
Azerbaidzjan	2.2	1.5	0.5	8.6	1.6
Lithuania	—	—	—	—	1.4
Moldova	—	—	0.4	—	1.9
Latvia	—	—	0.3	—	0.7
Kirgizstan	0.03	0.01	—	0.8	0.8
Tadzjikistan	0.04	0.03	—	10.8	1.5
Armenia	—	—	—	—	1.1
Turkmenistan	0.9	11.5	—	15.1	0.3
Estonia	—	—	—	—	2.4

	TV sets	Fridges	Grain	Milk	GNP
Russia	45.3	56.0	52.7	51.8	61.1
Ukraine	35.6	13.5	24.3	22.7	16.2
Belarus	10.8	11.3	3.5	7.0	4.2
Uzbekistan	—	2.7	1.1	2.7	3.3
Kazakhstan	—	—	11.6	5.0	4.3
Georgia	0.6	—	0.4	0.7	1.6
Azerbaidzjan	—	5.7	0.7	1.0	1.7
Lithuania	6.8	5.6	1.6	3.0	1.4
Moldova	0.9	2.5	1.6	1.4	1.2
Latvia	—	2.7	0.7	1.8	1.1
Kirgizstan	—	—	0.9	1.0	0.8
Tadzjikistan	—	—	0.2	0.5	0.8
Armenia	—	—	0.2	0.5	0.9
Turkmenistan	—	—	0.2	0.4	0.7
Estonia	—	—	0.3	1.2	0.6

Source: Goskomstat (1989b: 340–3, 454, 459, 487)

lisation certain branches of industry were developed preferentially in selected areas. Such concentrated branches are observed in metallurgy, machine building and chemical industries, which are characteristic of modern industrialisation. The less developed republics show an industrial structure with certain highly specialised branches based on natural deposits and on the traditional sectors of manufacturing: light industry and food industries. Yet, in the course of the general industrialisation of the whole country, the trend has been towards more complex development, where the less developed republics have been catching up with regard to modern branches of industry. A special Soviet feature of this normal regional development pattern might be seen in the balanced distribution of the energy and construction materials sectors (Wagener 1973: 69).

Wagener tested whether the pattern of specialisation as he found it was in accordance with Hekscher–Ohlin's Theorem. Assuming that the general characterisation of regions does not change over a certain period, one should expect the structure of regional economies to show a tendency towards capital-intensive branches in the more developed regions and towards labour-intensive branches in the less developed regions (Wagener 1973: 78). Although the empirical difficulties in the study were manifold, his results 'may constitute some weak support for the theory' (Wagener 1973: 79).

THE UNION'S INFRASTRUCTURAL LEGACY

Sixty-nine years of the Soviet Union led to a specialised pattern of production as described above, and also to an infrastructure that facilitated an exchange of products as required by the division of labour. Rail and pipeline networks together accounted for 83 per cent of all freight shipments in 1990, as can be seen from Table 3.8. Trucks in the CIS operate mainly in and around cities; their average length of haul is only 21 kilometres (Hunter 1994: 598). The dominant role of railway and pipeline networks has important future consequences, because flows of goods that were transported

Table 3.8 Transport in the USSR by mode, 1990 (as a percentage of total; freight in ton-kilometres, passengers in passenger-kilometres)

	Freight	*Passengers*
Rail	46.2	46.6
Gas pipe	20.5	0.0
Oil pipe	16.2	0.0
Maritime	12.4	0.0
Internal water	2.9	0.7
Road	1.7	17.1
Air	0.0	35.5

Source: Hunter (1994: 599, 601)

via these networks cannot easily be redirected towards new trade partners.

The territorial principle in the distribution of former Soviet property, discussed in the previous chapter, has also been applied to these networks. Today Kazakhstan's oil export route, the pipe-line to Novorossysk on the Black Sea, is controlled by a Russian monopoly, Rosnefttransport. The Russians themselves face similar problems, because of the nine oil pipeline outlets in the west, only three are in Russia, one in the White Sea and two in the Black Sea. Georgia and Ukraine also have an outlet in the Black Sea, and Latvia and Lithuania both have an outlet in the Baltic Sea. Furthermore one line passes through Ukraine before it continues into Eastern Europe, and another passes through Belarus. The lines that pass through Baku (in Azerbaidzjan) and Grozny (the Chechen capital) are in very unstable areas and are therefore of limited use.

CONCLUSION

This chapter characterised the former Soviet republics and the Union that existed among them from a historical, demographic, juridical, geographic and cultural point of view. Factor endow-ments per republic and the republics' produce were described, and the physical links among their economies were briefly touched upon. We can conclude from this chapter that the cultural and geographical diversity and the centralisation of power within the Soviet Union were huge. Very different peoples and lands were held together by a very strong centre. The economies of the republics were highly specialised and integrated via an extensive rail and pipeline infrastructure. In the next chapter, we further analyse and document the degree of economic integration as it existed among the republics by studying the cross-border move-ments of both factors and goods.

4

FORMER SOVIET REPUBLICS' ECONOMIC INTERDEPENDENCE

INTRODUCTION

This chapter analyses the economic interdependencies that existed among the republics of the former USSR. We show that the level of economic cooperation among the republics was high. The former Soviet republics traded heavily among each other and little with the rest of the world. This high degree of economic integration was caused by the fact that the Soviet Union was a planned economy with a single planning centre. Now that this centre has disappeared and the Soviet Union has broken up, much less intense economic relations among the republics can be expected, and much more trade with the outside world can also be expected. The next chapter attempts to assess future trade flows on the basis of a gravity model. In this chapter we describe the situation as it existed before the fall of Communism. A comparison of the two chapters can be used subsequently to describe what the effects of break-up on the exchange of goods and factors can be expected to be. We describe interrepublican flows of goods, capital and labour as they took place in the former Soviet Union in the third, fourth and fifth sections respectively. On these premises, we subsequently try to indicate future trends in the sixth section. We start by explaining in the next section some of the main difficulties in analysing Soviet economic interrepublican relations.

ANALYSING SOVIET REPUBLICS' ECONOMIC INTERDEPENDENCE

Analysing the economic interdependence of former Soviet republics is far more complicated than analysing, for example, the economic interdependence of the states of the USA. The main problem in the Soviet case is that intra-USSR relative prices and units of account are different from extra-USSR relative prices and units of account. Conversely, in analysing the interdependence among the states, intra-USA units of account (dollars) can easily be related to units of account that measure extra-USA economic relations (also dollars or currencies that are linked to the dollar via a market exchange rate). Similarly, intra-USA and extra-USA relative prices can be assumed to be not too divergent; both these relative prices are governed by market conditions, and in the absence of barriers to trade and other market imperfections, they should be the same. For this reason, the flow of Californian exports to Mexico on the one hand and to Texas on the other can easily be compared, added, or subtracted as one pleases. By contrast, comparing, adding or subtracting the flow of Estonian exports to the Ukraine on the one hand and to France on the other is a hazardous matter.

The problem of relating Soviet republics' intra-USSR economic relations to their relations with the non-Soviet world recurs throughout this chapter. The Soviet statistics available allow three different options to solve this problem; all three are applied, but they lead to results that should be interpreted differently. Goskomstat (the Soviet statistical agency) publications present republics' intra-USSR and extra-USSR exchange separately for 1988. Both flows are expressed in two different ways: using internal prices and internal units of account (internal roubles, IRs) and using 'world market prices' and external units of account ('valuta roubles', VRs). This implies that we can combine intra-USSR and extra-USSR exchange either by using the same prices and units of account for both flows (internal prices and IRs are applied in the next section, whereas 'world market prices' and VRs are applied in the penultimate section), or by using an IR/VR exchange rate (the fourth section). The nature of the problem under observation (1988 goods flows in the third section, capital flows in the fourth section, and future goods flows in the sixth section) determines the best solution to the problem of combining intra-USSR and extra-USSR flows.

Goskomstat's subdivision of Soviet republics' exchange in two flows (intra-USSR and extra-USSR) is a significant simplification of actual 1988 exchange and trade practices. The units of account and the relative prices of intra-CMEA (Council of Mutual Economic Assistance) trade are comparable to Soviet trade with market economies only as far as intra-CMEA trade in 'hard' goods is concerned (a 'hard' good is a homogeneous good for which a world market price can easily be determined, such as oil). Soviet trade with market economies was conducted in convertible currencies; these currencies were converted into VRs for bookkeeping purposes using the 'official' exchange rate (1.63 US dollar/VR in 1988).[1] Intra-CMEA hard goods trade used five-year moving averages of world market prices, converted into 'transferable roubles' (TRs) via the same official exchange rate (Lavigne 1985: 157). This implies, for example, that the price of oil in Soviet trade with market economies in 1988 (in VRs) would have been equal to the price of oil in intra-CMEA transactions (in TRs) if the price of oil had been stable from 1983 to 1988, or if the average world market price over this period was equal to the 1988 world market price. Removing from the problem the fact that a sliding average of world market prices instead of actual world market prices was used in intra-CMEA trade, in this context of 'hard' goods exchange there is no difference between TRs and VRs.

However, some goods that were traded among CMEA member states (such as Trabants) were not traded with or among market economies, and it is very difficult to determine a 'world market price' for these so-called 'soft' goods. Intra-CMEA trade in these goods was simply barter, and TR values were decided arbitrarily to give an impression of the magnitude of this barter. It is not clear how this intra-CMEA soft goods exchange (which is a significant part of total extra-USSR exchange) has been accounted for in the Goskomstat statistics mentioned above. Probably, it was simply awarded a certain TR value and subsequently added to VRs from trade with the West and TRs from intra-CMEA hard goods exchange.

The predicate 'arbitrary' has also often been given to internal Soviet prices (in IRs). These prices were not the result of the free interplay of market forces, but were set by the Union government, so that it is unclear whether these prices expressed relative scarcities. Soviet internal relative prices were certainly quite different from world market relative prices. Yet this does not imply that they were completely arbitrary. As we shall see in the next section, the former USSR was a relatively closed economic system, implying that Soviet scarcity conditions were unlikely to be equal to world market scarcity conditions. In calculating Soviet republics' GNPs (also in the next section), we shall assume that Soviet IR prices can be taken as an expression of Soviet relative scarcity.

Another potential arbitrary factor in our analysis is the use of the official exchange rate to relate VRs to IRs (the fourth section). In 1988, the official rate mentioned above was also the rate at which foreign tourists could legally exchange their hard currency for roubles. On the streets of Moscow, many more roubles could be obtained for a dollar. To stop this practice, a 'special' tourist rate of six roubles per dollar was introduced in November 1989. This solved the problem only partially, for the black market exchange rate remained substantially more favourable to the foreign tourist in 1990. From this evidence, it could easily be concluded that the official exchange rate 'overvalued' the rouble. Yet, the number of roubles obtained by foreigners in exchange for dollars on the streets of Moscow seems to be rather piecemeal evidence for the hypothesis that the official exchange rate put too high a value on the rouble.

How do we know if a currency is overvalued? For a market economy with a fixed exchange rate, we would conclude that its currency is overvalued if its balance of payments is in deficit for a prolonged period. Unfortunately, because of the Soviet central government's foreign trade monopoly, we do not have such a test here. Alternatively, we could adopt a purchasing power parity (PPP) criterion. If we assert that the official exchange rate is not in line with PPP, we implicitly accuse the Soviet authorities of having made an error, because they claimed to have set the official exchange rate on the basis of a PPP criterion. A sufficient condition for rouble overvaluation would be: all commodities have higher internal prices (in IRs) than external prices, the latter being obtained by multiplying a dollar price by the overvalued dollar/VR exchange rate. This condition was not met in 1988. Take, for example, the price of oil. In 1988, the internal price of oil was 30 IR per ton. The average world market price for 1988 was 124.1 dollars per ton. Via the official exchange rate, this translates into a rouble price of 76.1 VR, which is higher than 30 IR. In the fourth section, we assume that the Soviet authorities have made a reasonable estimate of the PPP exchange rate. This allows us to add interrepublican commodity flows to external Soviet trade, expressed in VRs.[2] In short, the analysis of Soviet interrepublican economic relations is hampered by a number of obstacles stemming from the peculiarities of the Soviet economic system. We shall encounter further difficulties in the more detailed study of particular problems that follows.

43

EXCHANGE OF OUTPUTS

A country's level of integration into the world economy can be expressed in a trade to GNP ratio ((exports+imports) divided by (2×GNP)). Here we try to calculate a similar ratio for the former Soviet republics.[3]

For the denominator, we take the republic net material product (NMP) multiplied by the Union GNP/NMP ratio.[4] Soviet national income accounting differs from Western practice. NMP, sometimes referred to as national income produced (NIP), is the sum of value added in the Soviet economy. It differs from GNP in that both depreciation and a large number of economic sectors, especially services, are not included. On the republican level, only NMP data are available, but for the Union both NMP and GNP data are published. Hence, we can calculate republican GNP figures by calculating the Union GNP/NMP ratio and multiplying the republican NMP data by this coefficient. This presupposes that the ratio of GNP to NMP is the same for all Soviet republics, which is not very likely. The share of services in the economy is related to economic development, and the levels of development of the republics are widely divergent. Yet, to avoid arbitrariness in the data, the best solution is to multiply all republican NMP data by the same Union GNP/NMP ratio for 1988.[5]

In the numerator, we must combine interrepublican and extra-USSR exchange of commodities. This is done by taking all exchange in domestic prices, because this is the only option available that renders extra-USSR exchange comparable to both intra-USSR exchange and to GNP as we have calculated it (also in internal prices). Only if we take all exchange in internal prices is a ton of Russian oil exported to Lithuania awarded the same value as a ton exported to France (namely, 30 IR); if we applied an exchange rate here (the official exchange rate or another rate that puts a lower value on the rouble), the value of the ton exported to France would be higher (at least 76 VR). We must use a single price vector to compare internal to external interdependence, and it must be the internal price vector, in order to obtain a meaningful trade to GNP ratio. The resulting ratios are presented in Table 4.1.

These ratios should be interpreted with some care. On top of the assumptions mentioned already, we will present a few more here. NMP was corrected for missing sectors, but we did not correct trade flows for the potential exclusion of trade in services because

Table 4.1 USSR trade to GNP ratios, 1988

| | Trade to GNP: | | | |
	Intra-Union (%)	Extra-Union (%)	Total (%)	Ratio of intra to extra
Russia	12.92	9.37	22.29	1.38
Ukraine	26.89	7.14	34.03	3.77
Belarus	44.54	7.38	51.93	6.03
Uzbekistan	34.08	5.62	39.70	6.06
Kazakhstan	29.47	4.69	34.15	6.28
Georgia	37.87	5.90	43.77	6.42
Azerbaidzjan	35.37	5.95	41.32	5.94
Lithuania	47.24	7.21	54.45	6.55
Moldova	45.86	6.36	52.22	7.21
Latvia	46.84	7.21	54.05	6.50
Kirgizstan	39.63	5.98	45.61	6.63
Tadzjikistan	36.17	5.76	41.94	6.28
Armenia	47.83	5.84	53.67	8.19
Turkmenistan	37.56	4.60	42.16	8.16
Estonia	50.09	8.79	58.88	5.70
USSR	21.10	8.27	29.37	2.55

Sources: Author's calculations from Vanous (1994: 6) for republican NMP data and Goskomstat (1990c: 11) for the Union GNP/NMP ratio; commodity exchange statistics from Goskomstat (1991: 14–15), all commodity exchange in internal Soviet prices

there are no data available on this. However, this may be a minor problem because there was probably little 'trade' among Soviet republics in services. Next, both the data on foreign trade flows and the national income statistics probably include turnover taxes. These taxes bias the data, for they are alternatively added to the value of the product at the point of consumption or at the point of production, thus introducing an arbitrary factor (Schiffer 1989: 105). Moreover, turnover taxes are not levied on most intermediate products. This implies that the NMP of producers of, say, consumer durables (the high turnover taxes on these are accounted for at the place of production, see Schiffer 1989: 107) is artificially raised relative to the NMP of raw material producers. These qualifications must be borne in mind when interpreting the data.

The significance of the data becomes especially clear when we compare the USSR with the European Union (EU) (Table 4.2). Measured in population, these two economic unions are about the same size (EU: 324.6 million vs USSR: 286.7 million). The level of

Table 4.2 EU trade to GNP ratios, 1988

| | Trade to GNP ratios: | | | |
	Intra-Union (%)	Extra-Union (%)	Total	Ratio of intra to extra
Belgium/Lux.	42.91	16.45	59.35	2.61
Denmark	12.97	12.11	25.08	1.07
FRG	12.81	11.02	23.83	1.10
Greece	10.73	6.30	17.03	1.70
Spain	8.56	6.16	14.73	1.40
France	11.88	6.86	18.73	1.73
Ireland	38.25	14.30	52.55	2.67
Italy	9.21	6.87	16.08	1.34
Netherlands	31.58	14.73	46.31	2.14
Portugal	22.48	10.40	32.88	2.16
UK	10.25	10.47	20.72	0.97
EU	13.38	9.37	22.75	1.43

Source: Author's calculations from Eurostat (1990: 37, 259)

external integration, expressed in ((imports + exports)/2×GNP), is also about equal (EU: 9.37 per cent; USSR: 8.27 per cent). They differ in their degree of internal integration, however.

From these data, we see that the overall level of integration of Soviet republics, when compared to EU member states, is higher. This reflects the high level of internal integration of the Soviet economy. The external integration for a Soviet republic is on average lower than that of an EU member state.

How can we account for this? A possible hypothesis is that the USSR was regionally 'overspecialised'. In a planned economy, the level of regional specialisation is a matter of planning; in the EU, it is the outcome of the free interplay of market forces. In this line of reasoning, the level of EU integration is efficient because it is brought about by the market. The USSR should have similar trade to GNP ratios, and if it has much higher internal ratios, it must be overspecialised. Indeed, a system that uses output as a success indicator (including the 'output' of transport kilometres!) and pays little attention to efficiency runs a serious risk of regional 'over-specialisation' in the sense that in the tradeoff between scale economies and transport costs, the former are overemphasised. However, yet other factors may cause the ratios for the EU and the USSR to differ, making the 'USSR overspecialisation' hypothesis unnecessary.

First, the trivial observation that fifteen republics are four more than eleven member states is relevant (Belgium and Luxemburg are treated as a single unit). The higher the degree of internal subdivision, the higher the degree of internal integration relative to external integration, simply because by making more internal subdivisions, internal trade rises whereas external trade is not affected. This, however, is partly compensated by the predominant weight of Russia within the USSR.

Second, impediments to intra-EU trade have been far from completely removed. Hence, on the basis of these data, it could be just as well argued that Soviet central planning chose the efficient level of specialisation, and that EU market forces have not led to the same level yet, because of remaining impediments.

Historically, the high degree of Soviet internal integration relative to its external integration can be explained by the failure of Soviet attempts to establish a significant division of labour within the CMEA group. For example, all East European economies developed their own heavy industry. The high degree of intra-USSR division of labour can be viewed as a compensation for this. The central government did have the power to tell the republics what to produce, and used it too.

Finally, it should be stressed that countries differ, groups of countries differ, and therefore the efficient rate of specialisation differs. On the basis of trade to GNP ratios, it can be argued that the USSR is *more* specialised regionally than the EU, but certainly not that it is *over*specialised.

EXCHANGE OF INPUTS: CAPITAL

Interrepublican (intra-USSR) capital flows cannot easily be compared with intra-EU capital flows, because they are completely different in nature: they are grants, not loans. In the former USSR, imbalances in goods exchange among republics did not lead to financial commitments. Thus, a Soviet republic could 'use' more than produce by importing more than exporting, without raising any debts. The resulting pattern of transfers has been studied by Wagener for 1965, by Gillula for 1966 (as well as for a smaller sample of republics for the 1960s and early 1970s), and by Belkindas and Sagers for the 1970s and 1980s. All studies concluded that the Central Asian republics were subsidised by the rest of the Union, the donors being mainly the Slavic republics (Wagener 1973: 99; Gillula 1979: 619; Belkindas and Sagers 1990: 629).

In these studies different methods are employed. The 'capital transfer' is equal to the 'trade balance' (the difference between the value of all goods and services that leave the republic and all that enter). If statistics on goods exchange are available they should be used to assess this balance directly. Unfortunately, the republican input–output tables necessary to obtain data on interrepublican goods exchange were constructed only once every five years (Belkindas and Sagers 1990: 648). National income accounting statistics can be used to obtain a time series of capital transfers.[6] Below we introduce some symbolic notation clarifying this.

The basic equation relevant here is:

$$NIP = NIU + L + B \qquad (4.1)$$

where NIP = National Income Produced
(see above);

NIU = National Income Used, i.e.
the sum of consumption and
investment;

L = losses in the economy due to
abandoned construction, natural
calamities and the like; and

B = trade balance.

NIP and NIU data are available year by year, so we can use these to obtain a time series for B. Unfortunately, in view of the fact that we do not know L, the difference between NIP and NIU can only be taken as an approximation of B. Also, it is unclear whether the B that is obtained via this method is really the B we are looking for.

Once more we encounter here the problem of adding intra-USSR and extra-USSR trade. Applying internal prices to all goods exchange is clearly unsatisfactory in assessing Soviet republics' trade balances, because this would lead to a total deficit for all republics taken together of 50 billion roubles, whereas in fact the Soviet trade balance was in surplus in 1988. This is caused by the fact that the intra-USSR relative price of Soviet exports to imports is lower than the extra-USSR relative price. Internal prices are not a good measure of value in exchange with the non-Soviet world. Similarly, extra-USSR prices are not an adequate measure of value in intra-USSR exchange. Once it is taken for granted that a republic is a part of a closed economic system, different price vectors should be applied to measure the value of intra-system and extra-system transactions, because intra-system scarcity conditions are different from extra-system scarcity conditions. Hence, the best method that can be used to assess the trade balance (and hence capital transfers) is to apply the official exchange rate (which is assumed to be a reasonable expression of PPP) so as to make the two flows comparable.

How does the trade balance that is obtained using the official exchange rate to make IRs and VRs comparable relate to B in equation (4.1)? That is quite unclear. Soviet statistical annuals (*Narkhoz*) present equation (4.1) for the Union as a whole, without defining what B is exactly.[7] If we apply this equation to a Soviet republic, the meaning of B becomes even more obscure, because now it should contain not only foreign trade flows but also inter-republican trade flows. We can conclude that it is very difficult to interpret (NIP − NIU), first because we must make an assumption about the distribution of L (for 1988, a distribution proportional to GNP seems inappropriate in view of the huge destruction that took place in Armenia because of an earthquake), and second because we do not know what the B that we can obtain really means. Yet a view of the 1988 data set indicates that B in equation (4.1) might not be too different from the trade balance that we deemed optimal for assessing capital transfers. Table 4.3 presents the relevant data.

Table 4.3 Trade and income balance, 1988 (million roubles)

Republic	Trade balance	Income balance (NIP − NIU)
Russia	7,230	10,500
Ukraine	2,310	5,400
Belarus	3,590	4,100
Uzbekistan	−1,570	−1,100
Kazakhstan	−6,040	−5,400
Georgia	−20	200
Azerbaidzjan	1,890	1,700
Lithuania	−1,170	−900
Moldova	−610	−500
Latvia	−420	−500
Kirgizstan	−1020	−1,000
Tadzjikistan	−940	−800
Armenia	−650	800
Turkmenistan	−160	−100
Estonia	−540	−500
Sum	+1,880	+11,900

Sources: Vanous (1992: 5) for national income balance, Goskomstat (1991: 14–15) for trade balance

Table 4.4 Capital transfers, 1966–91 (% of GNP)

	1966	1967	1968	1969	1970
Russia	3.4	5.1	6.6	7.7	8.6
Ukraine	8.9	7.4	6.1	4.9	3.9
Belarus	−1.0	−0.3	0.2	0.7	1.0
Uzbekistan	−15.5	−13.4	−11.5	−9.9	−8.5
Kazakhstan	−38.1	−31.3	−25.4	−20.1	−15.6
Georgia	−7.6	−7.2	−6.8	−6.5	−6.1
Azerbaidzjan	0.3	0.4	0.5	0.6	0.7
Lithuania	16.9	21.2	24.5	27.2	29.1
Moldova	11.6	9.8	8.2	6.7	5.5
Latvia	7.9	6.2	4.7	3.4	2.2
Kirgizstan	−15.6	−14.0	−12.5	−11.2	−10.0
Tadzjikistan	−18.1	−15.1	−12.0	−9.4	−7.1
Armenia	−8.0	−7.2	−6.5	−5.9	−5.3
Turkmenistan	−17.8	−10.9	−5.2	−0.6	3.1
Estonia	1.4	0.7	0.1	−0.4	−0.9

	1971	1972	1973	1974	1975
Russia	7.9	7.2	6.5	5.7	5.0
Ukraine	4.4	4.4	8.0	7.1	4.6
Belarus	5.8	8.1	11.3	12.5	16.0
Uzbekistan	−4.3	−7.0	−5.1	−4.3	−1.8
Kazakhstan	−13.2	−9.7	−11.4	−16.5	−24.3
Georgia	−5.9	−11.9	−10.8	−4.8	−3.0
Azerbaidzjan	4.6	3.7	8.2	6.8	8.1
Lithuania	28.6	28.1	25.3	26.7	24.5
Moldova	5.4	5.3	5.2	5.1	5.0
Latvia	4.2	6.2	2.1	6.2	6.1
Kirgizstan	−6.8	−8.9	−11.9	−13.6	−15.6
Tadzjikistan	−7.6	−8.0	−8.4	−8.8	−9.3
Armenia	−10.3	−1.1	−3.4	2.1	3.7
Turkmenistan	0.0	−2.1	5.1	8.0	10.4
Estonia	−1.8	0.2	−3.3	0.0	−0.2

	1976	1977	1978	1979	1980
Russia	4.3	3.5	2.8	2.0	1.3
Ukraine	7.1	8.0	8.5	5.9	3.9
Belarus	16.7	16.8	19.1	16.8	14.9
Uzbekistan	−3.0	−3.6	−5.6	−5.4	−5.3
Kazakhstan	−11.8	−22.9	−18.1	−15.4	−15.6
Georgia	−3.1	−1.3	0.3	4.8	3.5
Azerbaidzjan	11.3	12.4	22.3	20.6	24.6
Lithuania	19.9	14.0	7.5	−1.1	−8.0
Moldova	5.9	7.4	6.9	6.7	5.9
Latvia	5.8	6.9	8.0	5.9	8.9

Table 4.4 (continued)

	1976	1977	1978	1979	1980
Kirgizstan	−15.4	−16.1	−13.8	−16.6	−13.1
Tadzjikistan	−9.7	−9.9	−10.6	−11.0	−11.5
Armenia	5.3	8.6	9.0	9.3	15.6
Turkmenistan	2.3	7.3	8.6	0.6	6.7
Estonia	3.7	0.8	0.4	−5.6	−4.3

	1981	1982	1983	1984	1985
Russia	1.3	1.3	1.3	1.3	1.2
Ukraine	6.0	7.5	6.8	5.8	5.0
Belarus	18.2	17.2	18.9	17.6	16.3
Uzbekistan	−3.1	−4.7	−5.9	−9.5	−4.1
Kazakhstan	−19.3	−20.2	−17.7	−29.1	−23.3
Georgia	11.0	12.0	5.3	4.7	3.4
Azerbaidzjan	23.8	22.6	23.4	20.0	22.4
Lithuania	−2.8	0.7	−0.7	−3.0	−6.0
Moldova	1.0	2.8	10.7	6.4	4.4
Latvia	5.8	6.2	4.0	3.4	2.3
Kirgizstan	−11.2	−10.0	1.3	−0.2	−9.2
Tadzjikistan	−10.6	−9.7	−8.8	−8.0	−7.1
Armenia	12.3	14.0	12.1	13.4	11.7
Turkmenistan	4.9	3.0	1.0	−0.9	−2.9
Estonia	−4.9	−5.6	−4.0	−6.0	−5.6

	1986	1987	1988	1989	1990	1991
Russia	1.7	2.1	2.5	3.6	3.6	4.7
Ukraine	3.5	3.6	5.0	1.0	−1.3	0.0
Belarus	12.3	13.7	15.8	11.0	3.4	4.3
Uzbekistan	−5.1	−7.6	−15.0	−14.4	−22.0	−20.6
Kazakhstan	−20.3	−20.6	−20.8	−21.4	−20.1	−18.8
Georgia	4.7	7.6	2.3	4.0	−7.3	−6.2
Azerbaidzjan	21.9	21.2	15.3	27.0	3.7	4.9
Lithuania	−6.0	−8.7	−10.2	−5.2	−7.0	−5.5
Moldova	0.3	−2.5	−5.4	−7.0	−3.2	−1.9
Latvia	0.6	−0.7	−6.8	−3.9	0.0	0.6
Kirgizstan	−13.3	−16.9	−20.0	−28.6	−21.7	−20.2
Tadzjikistan	−9.2	−11.4	−13.6	−21.3	−9.1	−7.2
Armenia	10.7	8.2	12.0	−5.8	−11.4	−10.0
Turkmenistan	−3.0	−3.0	−3.1	−8.2	−3.8	−3.3
Estonia	−6.2	−6.5	−12.9	−13.6	−12.7	−11.5

Sources: Author's calculations from income statistics presented by Belkindas and Sagers (1990: 636) for 1970–88; from Vanous (1992) for 1989–91. In order to obtain similar data for 1966–9 we interpolated between 1965 transfer data from Wagener (1973) and data from Belkindas and Sagers (1990) for 1970

It turns out that (NIP − NIU) is a very good proxy for B: the coefficient of correlation is 97 per cent.[8] A significant 'sign problem' exists only for Armenia, but this can be easily explained in view of the huge destruction that took place in this republic in 1988 on account of the earthquake. The sum of (NIP − NIU) is higher than the sum of B, as it should be, because of L. If (NIP − NIU) can be viewed as a reasonable proxy for the trade balance as defined above, we can take the available 1970–88 data set to obtain a time series. The resulting capital transfers are presented in Table 4.4.

We see that there is some basic stability in the pattern of transfers. Over most of the period 1966–91, Russia, Ukraine, Belarus, Azerbaidzjan are donors, whereas Uzbekistan, Kazakhstan, Kirgizstan and Tadzjikistan are receivers. The pattern of interrepublican capital transfers and its effects on the republics' level of income is studied further in Chapter 8.

EXCHANGE OF INPUTS: LABOUR

How do interrepublican capital transfers relate to interrepublican transfers of labour? Table 4.5 presents the relevant migration statistics.

The basic migration patterns can be summarised as follows. The

Table 4.5 Absolute net migration by republic, 1959–95 (thousands)

	1959–70	1970–79	1979–87	1989–95
Russia	−1,700.0	200.0	1,442.7	1,716.0
Ukraine	500.0	300.0	−26.4	453.0
Belarus	−287.0	−89.0	−3.2	65.0
Uzbekistan	514.0	135.0	−246.4	−1,065.0
Kazakhstan	795.0	−464.0	−504.6	−565.0
Georgia	−92.0	−136.0	−144.1	−230.0
Azerbaidzjan	−58.0	−62.0	−207.9	−335.0
Lithuania	51.0	66.0	92.2	−24.0
Moldova	63.0	−23.0	−112.0	−143.0
Latvia	158.0	104.0	78.4	−142.0
Kirgizstan	161.0	−79.0	−96.9	−359.0
Tadzjikistan	69.0	41.0	−70.2	−235.0
Armenia	146.0	111.0	−79.6	32.0
Turkmenistan	13.0	−13.0	−57.8	315.0
Estonia	92.5	60.0	50.6	−82.0

Source: Rowland (1988: 812) for 1959–87; Heleniak (1995: 2) for 1989–1995

most mobile ethnic group in the former USSR was the Slavic, and especially the Russian population. In the 1960s, both Central Asia and the Baltics experienced Russian in-migration. This trend was reversed for Central Asia in the 1980s, but not for the Baltics. Thus, the capital that flowed into the peripheral republics was accompanied by Russian labour inflow in the 1960s. An interesting question is whether Russian labour was transferred to peripheral republics in order to facilitate the creation of local industries or if local industries were set up in order to facilitate the inflow of Russians in the peripheral republics. Was the aim of the operation really to equalise levels of economic development among the republics, or was it to create a political stronghold in the peripheral republics? Many Soviets would opt for the latter interpretation.

In Central Asia, in the 1980s, there was still a capital inflow, but there was a labour outflow. The conclusion seems to be that the jobs created by capital inflow in Central Asia were first filled by Russians and later taken over by the indigenous population, which was made possible by the high rate of natural increase in the Central Asian republics. In the Baltic republics, inflow of Russians has often been connected to huge investment projects as well (the Mazeikiai oil refinery, the Ignalina nuclear power station). Yet, this makes it difficult to account for the net in-migration in the 1960s and 1970s, as the Baltic region experienced a net capital outflow in this period. The higher standards of living in these republics might account for the inflow of Russians in this period.

Migration patterns since the break-up of the USSR are to a large extent the consequence of persons moving to the republic of their titular nationality. Because of the numbers involved, the dominant flow is that of Russians back to Russia. As stated, the 'Russian retreat' from Central Asia started long before the break-up. Soviet break-up accelerated rather than initiated this process, as can be seen from the increased emigration from Tadzjikistan, Kirgizstan and especially Uzbekistan (in the last column of Table 4.5). In the case of the Baltic republics, Soviet break-up reversed the existing migration trend. In the period 1959–87 Estonia, Latvia and Lithuania experienced net immigration, whereas in the period 1989–95 net emigration can be observed. This reverse is caused by Russians on the move (Heleniak 1995: 2). By the end of 1995, about 10 per cent of Russians living in the 'near abroad' had returned to Russia, and the same is true for most other ethnic groups (Heleniak 1995: 5). This implies that a large potential for migration among the republics that is caused by ethnic factors remains.

INTERREPUBLICAN ECONOMIC RELATIONS: FUTURE PROSPECTS

Future trade among independent Soviet republics will surely be conducted in prices that are determined by world market scarcity conditions, not by Soviet scarcity conditions. Hence, it is interesting to recalculate interrepublican trade in world market prices, and both Goskomstat and observers in the West have done so (Goskomstat 1991: 14–15; Hanson 1990: 45). Table 4.6 presents the results of Goskomstat's recalculation.

Comparing these trade balances to those in the first column in Table 4.3, we see that a switch to world market prices in interrepublican trade adversely affects the trade balance of all republics except Russia and Turkmenistan. Generally, the Central Asian republics suffer less from a switch to world market prices than the non-Russian European republics. This can easily be explained: the intra-Union relative price of raw materials to consumer goods was lower than the extra-Union relative price, and the Russian

Table 4.6 Trade balance to GNP, 1988 (million roubles)

Republic	Trade balance	Percentage of GNP
Russia	30,840	5.77
Ukraine	−2,890	−2.03
Belarus	−2,050	−5.64
Uzbekistan	−2,540	−8.84
Kazakhstan	−6,580	−17.63
Georgia	−1,910	−13.49
Azerbaidzjan	−450	−2.97
Lithuania	−3,690	−29.88
Moldova	−2,630	−24.61
Latvia	−1,310	−13.49
Kirgizstan	−1,060	−15.28
Tadzjikistan	−1,120	−16.14
Armenia	−1,370	−17.02
Turkmenistan	40	0.61
Estonia	−1,300	−22.85

Source: Goskomstat (1991: 14–15), all trade measured in world market prices. These data are practically equal to those calculated by the CEC (1990a: table 25, column 7)

Federation was the main producer and exporter of raw materials in the USSR; the Central Asian republics also produced and exported these goods, but to a lesser extent.

Obviously, changing the price structure would also change the structure of goods exchange among republics; therefore, as a prediction of future trade imbalances these figures are not very good. Moreover, a serious problem exists with the ratios presented in the second column of this table because the denominator is still measured in internal prices. However, if calculated correctly, they do give an indication of the huge changes in the current pattern of goods exchange that are necessary to achieve a minimum amount of equilibrium on the republics' trade balances, because the trade deficits are extremely high for many republics. For 1989, trade deficits of notorious debtors like Brazil, Mexico and Poland of some 20–70 per cent of GNP are reported (World Bank 1991). If prices and flows of goods were to remain the same, some of the republics would reach a similar ratio in a single year!

Once more, a warning regarding the reliability of Goskomstat's data should be given here. Goskomstat's explanatory notes to the figures on the effects of a switch to world market prices in intra-USSR exchange raise some doubts on exactly what 'world market' was used to derive 'world market prices'. For example, Goskomstat claims that the price of oil on the world market is a factor of 3.3 higher than the intra-Union oil price; the world market price of meat is a factor of 3.1 lower (Goskomstat 1990b: 50). This is not in line with available data on these prices. Yet, it is true that the intra-USSR relative meat-to-oil price was lower than the extra-USSR price.[9] On the basis of this piecemeal evidence on the prices of meat and oil, we can venture the conclusion that Goskomstat's recalculation of intra-USSR exchange in world market prices leads to a change in the republics' trade balances (comparing the first column of Table 4.3 and the first column of Table 4.6) in the right direction, but that possibly overstates the effects of the switch.

We can conclude that the imbalances arising from the application of world market prices to intra-USSR exchange renders the 1988 structure of interrepublican goods exchange unsustainable. The deficit republics must either increase their exports or reduce their imports. In the short run, reducing imports is easier than increasing exports. Hence, the level of goods exchange can be expected to decline.

And indeed this is what has happened since the break-up of the

USSR. Michalopoulos and Tarr (1994: 3) estimate that trade among the republics in 1993 was at least 65 per cent lower than goods exchange among the republics in 1990. Their information suggests that trade between Russia and the republics declined over that period by 64 per cent, and trade among the other republics by 71.5 per cent. Of course, the existing imbalances in interrepublican goods exchange are only one of the possible explanations for the decline in interrepublican exchange. The general decline in economic activity should be mentioned here. Moreover, the change from one planned economy to a number of market economies implies some causes for a decline in goods exchange. Under the *ancien régime*, marketing costs were non-existent, whereas in a market setting the costs of selling a product in a different republic can be quite high. Next, transportation costs were artificially low in the old USSR. Finally, the old system was quite closed; trade reorientation takes place now that the former Soviet Union has opened up to the world economy.

On the future of interrepublican capital flows we can be brief: they will come to a halt. At present, all former Soviet republics are having a very hard time and are not in a position to grant capital to other republics; new capital must be imported from abroad. A central government that governs interrepublican goods exchange and thereby redistributes capital no longer exists. In the process of transition, however, some 'subsidies' caused by sticky prices might remain. For example, in January 1992 the Russian government decided not to liberalise oil prices, in fear of the disruptive effects such a move could have on Russian industry. For some time other non-oil-producing republics benefited from this measure. Because they obtained their oil for prices lower than market prices, they received a 'subsidy' or a 'capital transfer'.[10] These remaining subsidies are disappearing over time as well, though.

As we already briefly discussed in the previous section, labour flows will certainly not come to a halt. The trend of ethnic groups moving back to their 'home' republic can be expected to continue. In this respect, the flow that is potentially by far the most significant is of course that of Russians back to Russia. Table 4.7 presents the distribution of Russians in the former USSR as of 1989, and also the distribution of the second largest group, the Ukrainians, in order to give an impression of the potential magnitude of these labour flows.

Not all these people are under immediate threat. At present, the

Table 4.7 Distribution of Russians and Ukrainians in the USSR, 1989
(thousands)

Republic	Russians	Ukrainians	Total population
Russia	119,866	4,363	147,400
Ukraine	11,356	37,419	51,707
Belarus	1,342	291	10,200
Uzbekistan	1,653	153	19,905
Kazakhstan	6,288	96	16,536
Georgia	341	52	5,443
Azerbaidzjan	392	32	7,038
Lithuania	344	45	3,690
Moldova	562	600	4,338
Latvia	906	92	2,680
Kirghizia	917	108	4,290
Tadzjikistan	388	41	5,190
Armenia	52	8	3,228
Turkmenistan	334	36	3,534
Estonia	475	48	1,573

Source: Schwarz (1991: 211)

position of Russians and Ukrainians is especially precarious in some Islamic republics (Uzbekistan, Tadzjikistan and Azerbaidzjan). A large part of the 2.6 million Slavs living in these republics at the time of the break-up of the USSR have returned to Russia or Ukraine already, as Table 4.5 indicated. The huge minorities of 1 million Tadzjiks in Uzbekistan and 1.2 million Uzbeks in Tadzjikistan also deserve mentioning here as sources of potential migration.

Another major determinant of migration is economic performance. The republics that are most successful in transforming their economies into a market economy will attract a labour inflow from their neighbours. This renders Russia a likely target republic for migration. Poor as economic conditions may be in Russia at present, the medium-term prospects for recovery are excellent in this republic when compared with the other republics of the former Soviet Union. The combined effect of relative affluence in Russia and feelings of displacement may, for example, cause a large part of the 6 million Russians living in Kazakhstan to move to Russia.

CONCLUSION

In this chapter we presented methods for assessing the former Soviet republics' level of interdependence. We focused on inter-republican flows of goods and capital and presented some data on migration among the republics in order to complete the picture. We found that the level of goods exchange was high, higher than, for example, among EU member states. Huge capital transfers took place within this system from the Slavic republics to the peripheral republics. Finally, substantial Russian migration to other Soviet republics in the 1960s has been followed by a retreat in the 1980s and 1990s.

The break-up of the Soviet Union has changed the existing patterns significantly. The level of interrepublican goods exchange is declining at a rapid pace. Partly, this decline can be explained by the imbalances that we found in interrepublican exchange when world market prices are applied to this exchange. Interrepublican capital flows are also in decline; only some implicit subsidies or capital transfers caused by artificially low prices (especially the price of oil) remain. Finally, labour flows are sure to increase. The collapse of the Soviet Union opened the lid of *Pandora's box*. It proved to be filled with economic divergence and ethnic conflict, causing people to return to their home republics.

In the chapter that follows, we continue our study of the economic interdependencies as they existed among the republics of the former Soviet Union via a so-called 'gravity model'. We apply this model also to estimate future trade intensities among the Newly Independent States. This is done so that we can compare the exchange of goods among the republics and the rest of the world as it existed under Communism with the situation that can be expected to develop in the absence of an institutional bias in favour of some trade partners. We show that there is a huge difference between the situation that was and the situation that is likely to arise. This is an important economic effect of the break-up of the Soviet Union.

5

A GRAVITY MODEL OF THE
FORMER SOVIET UNION

INTRODUCTION

In this chapter we continue our analysis of the degree of integration of the Soviet economy. An analysis of goods exchange among
the republics in 1990, applying the gravity model in the third
section, leads to interesting results. The percentage of exchange
that can be explained by using only GNPs and distance as independent variables is much higher than in trade among market
economies, whereas the coefficient that is found for distance is
clearly lower. Both these observations point to a high degree of
internal economic integration.

Subsequently, in the second part of the chapter (the fourth
section) we use equations obtained from gravity analysis to 'fore-
cast' future exchange both among the republics themselves *and*
with the rest of the world. We then find that in the absence of an
institutional bias in favour of some trade partners (such as being
united in a single state, or being in a Customs Union together),
trade among the republics will be dwarfed by trade between the
republics and third countries. When they were parts of a single
state, the republics intensively exchanged goods. As independent
states, they are unlikely to continue to do this.

This result has some significant policy implications. The intensity
of trade relations is an important indicator of the potential success
of Customs Unions and Monetary Unions. This topic is discussed
briefly in the penultimate section, and more extensively when we
discuss the theory of Customs Unions and Monetary Unions in
Chapter 6.

59

GRAVITY MODELLING IN ECONOMICS

Sir Isaac Newton's law of gravity states that the attractive force between two bodies is proportional to the product of the masses of the two bodies, divided by the square of the distance between them. It took an economist who started his career as a physicist, the Dutch Nobel Laureate Jan Tinbergen, to introduce this idea into economics (Tinbergen *et al.* 1962). He suggested that trade between two countries can be explained by taking the mass of the countries, expressed in their GNPs, and the distance between them as explanatory variables. In subsequent econometric studies that applied the gravity method, many other explanatory variables have been added to improve the statistical results, such as population sizes and the existence of a common border. In this study, we stick to the two basic Newtonian variables.

The simple logic behind the gravity model is that exports are related to productive capacity and imports are related to consumptive capacities. Hence, the larger the GNPs of the two countries involved, the larger the trade. Trade is negatively correlated to distance, because of transport costs and the 'economic horizon'. People are better informed about conditions prevailing in nearby countries, such as laws, institutions, habits, language and way of life.

The 'economic horizon' factors do not apply to the Soviet case. Interrepublican goods exchange was decided by the planners in Moscow, who did not care about different languages or cultures. This might be the explanation for the fact that the distance coefficient that we found in our analysis of former Soviet interrepublican exchange was low according to international standards, as we shall see in the next section below.

THE SOVIET CASE

In our analysis of interrepublican exchange in the former Soviet Union, we use data that were published in two recent World Bank publications: Michalopoulos and Tarr (1992: 42) for exchange among the republics in 1990, and World Bank (1992: 4–5) for GNP data, also for 1990. For distance, we simply took the distance between the capitals of the republics as the crow flies. This is problematic, and we shall return to it below.

We estimated using the ordinary least squares equation

$$\ln(\text{trade}_{ij}) = \text{constant} + \alpha_1 \ln(\text{GNP}_i) + \alpha_2 \ln(\text{GNP}_j) + \alpha_3 \ln(\text{distance}) \qquad (5.1)$$

where trade_{ij} = goods from republic i to j; GNP_i = the national product of the 'exporting' republic; and GNP_j = national product of the importing republic. This is the usual formulation of the gravity equation in economics. The GNPs of the importer and the exporter are separated, because different motives are supposed to underlie a country's propensity to import or export. However, in the Soviet context such a distinction is in fact irrelevant, because flows of goods between republics were planned from Moscow. Therefore, we also estimated the equation

$$\ln(\text{trade}_{ij}^{*}) = \text{constant} + \alpha_1 \ln(\text{GNP}_i \times \text{GNP}_j) + \alpha_2 \ln(\text{distance}) \qquad (5.2)$$

where trade_{ij}^{*} = an average of imports and exports between i and j. The results of both estimations are presented in Table 5.1.

The adjusted R^2 of 0.96 implies that 96 per cent of interrepublican goods exchange can be explained by the sizes of the economies involved and the distances between them. The fact that the model fits a little less well when importers are separated from exporters can be attributed to the fact that some bilateral balances are highly unbalanced. For example, the reported exports from Azerbaidzjan to Turkmenistan in 1990 are 156.1 million roubles, whereas the reverse flow is reported to be only 15.6 million roubles. The latter value is so low that its correctness should be doubted. By taking the average of these two figures, however, the extremes are moderated.

The distance problem can be illustrated by taking the example of

Table 5.1 Results from the Soviet gravity model

	Equation (5.1)	Equation (5.2)
Observations	210	105
Constant	−7.77 (−14.77)	4.28 (13.42)
GNP_i, GNP_j	0.90 (32.66), 0.84 (30.59)	0.86 (45.84)
Distance	−0.59 (−14.04)	−0.58 (−14.81)
Adjusted R^2	0.92	0.96

Values calculated using TSP version 7.0. The *t*-values of the coefficients are added in parenthesis.

goods exchange between Uzbekistan and Turkmenistan. This is the pair with the largest difference between actual value and value fitted according to equation (5.2). Even though these two republics share a common border of more than a thousand kilometres, the model we apply puts them far apart. The *Atlas Avtomobilnij Dorog SSSR* (USSR Motorway Atlas) reports a distance of 1,294 kilometres between Ashkhabad and Tashkent. By taking air (crow) distances, we arrived at 1,035 kilometres. Hence, the fact that estimated trade, using this distance, is so much lower than actual trade should not come as a surprise.

Notwithstanding these difficulties, the model works extremely well in the former Soviet economy. This same result was obtained by Gros and Dautrebande (1992), who used a 1987 data set. We can put the results in context by comparing them to results obtained in similar studies. Table 5.2 lists seven such studies.

From these data, we can conclude that both the present study and the analysis by Gros and Dautrebande show that Soviet inter-republican goods exchange fits the pattern prescribed by gravity much better than trade between market economies. Moreover, the distance coefficient found in the two studies is lower than the coefficient usually found in trade among market economies. Our results imply that doubling the distance leads to a reduction of trade of only 33 per cent. This fact can be attributed to the underestimation of transport costs by the Soviet planners, but alternatively it can be argued that the 'economic horizon' factor is absent in the Soviet case, so that in fact the pattern found in the

Table 5.2 Results from gravity analyses compared

	Countries	Adj. R^2	Coefficient for distance
Wang/Winters	76	0.70	−0.75
Vjugin/Vavilov	19	0.90	−0.57
Linnemann	80	0.79	−0.81
van Bergeyk/Oldersma	40	0.65	−1.03
Biessen	27	0.60	−0.76
Bergstrand	15	0.79	−0.81
Among the fifteen Soviet republics:			
Gros/Dautrebande	15	0.92	−0.39

Sources: Wang and Winters (1992: 13, 27); Vjugin and Vavilov (1992: Appendix A); Gros and Dautrebande (1992: 11); Linnemann (1966: 82); van Bergeyk and Oldersma (1990: 62); Biessen (1991: 30, 32, 34); Bergstrand (1985: 475)

Soviet Union is more efficient than the pattern found in trade between market economies.

EXPECTED TRADE REORIENTATION

The gravity approach can be used to assess 'natural' trade intensities. This is especially useful in the Soviet context, since trade with the outside world was limited in the Soviet era. Most of the external trade that did take place was with CMEA partners. The pattern that existed was determined politically, not economically. Hence, the existing pattern is a very bad estimator of future patterns.

Other methods that have been developed for this purpose are of no avail. Collins and Rodrik (1991) take the 1928 situation as 'natural'. They predict the external trade of East European countries on the basis of the pattern that existed in 1928, correcting for the fact that some economies have grown faster than others. This approach cannot be applied to the case of the Soviet Union, both because, in the interwar period, the economic system of the USSR was closed to the outside world so that the 1928 situation can by no means be considered 'natural', and also because no extra-USSR trade data are available on a republican level. Goods exchange between, for example, Ukraine and the UK in 1928 is unknown. Hence, we must proceed differently, and we can by using the gravity approach.

It should be made clear from the beginning that an estimation of future trade patterns obtained via the gravity model is not very precise. The model concentrates on geography, completely ignoring history as well as traditional trade theory. Concepts such as comparative advantage, factor endowments, or – more modern – increasing returns to scale are banned from the analysis. Moreover, only a very small part of geography is taken. Mountains, rivers, seas and climate are all ignored. Yet the survey of Table 5.2 shows that the gravity approach works reasonably well for different sets of countries.

To limit data collection requirements, we estimate the former Soviet republics' trade with the USA (including Canada), the EU (including Sweden and Switzerland), Japan (including South Korea) and China (mainly because it seems particularly relevant for the Central Asian republics, especially if it continues its current rate of economic growth). These four flows combined were supposed to reflect trade with the 'rest of the world'.

The main problem in an analysis with both Western and Eastern data is how to make these data comparable. A rouble/dollar exchange rate is required to be able to compare the sizes in productive and consumptive capacities of the areas involved. Therefore, an exchange rate that is more or less in line with purchasing power parity (PPP) should be taken. The so-called 'official' exchange rate was supposed to be an expression of PPP. For 1990, we have two official rates, because the Soviet authorities changed the rate from 0.63 roubles per dollar to 1.80 roubles per dollar in November 1990 (Marer 1992: 239). We apply the second here, because we think that the authorities had good reason to change the rate, i.e. that the rate of 1.80 roubles per dollar is much more appropriate than the pre-November rate. Other candidate exchange rates are 6 roubles/dollar (the 1990 official tourist exchange rate) or 20 roubles/dollar (the rate on the streets of Moscow in 1990). Applying such exchange rates implies that non-Soviet GNPs are increased relative to Soviet GNPs, leading to predicted shifts in the pattern of external trade of the former Soviet republics that are even larger than the shifts described below.

We calculated the regional distribution of external trade for the Newly Independent States using the results from four 'gravity' regressions: the results found for equation (5.2) in this chapter, plus results obtained by Bergstrand (1985), Wang and Winters (1992) and Linneman (1966) (Table 5.3). Application of equation (5.2) leads to the largest predicted shift from intra-FSU trade to extra-FSU trade. The reason for this is the low coefficient for distance that was found in intra-FSU trade. If this coefficient is applied to predict future trade patterns, trade with long-distance partners is probably overestimated. Therefore, we also calculated a predicted regional distribution of external trade using the coefficients of three studies that analysed trade between market economies and had more normal distance coefficients. The results are somewhat less extreme, but the predicted shift in external trade is still very substantial.

Recent data confirm that these predictions might not be too far off the mark. For example, for Estonia this analysis indicates that 85 per cent of 'foreign' trade was with the other Soviet republics in the Communist era, whereas in the most conservative estimation

Table 5.3 Intra-USSR trade as a percentage of total trade

	Predicted van Selm	Bergstrand	Wang/Winters	Linneman
Russia	6.6	18.2	9.6	10.7
Ukraine	11.6	29.5	18.4	16.4
Belarus	14.5	36.1	23.1	20.7
Uzbekistan	10.2	19.8	10.7	13.9
Kazakhstan	9.4	21.4	12.7	12.7
Georgia	11.5	26.0	16.0	15.8
Azerbaidzjan	10.6	23.4	14.0	13.9
Lithuania	14.0	32.2	19.3	19.9
Moldova	12.6	23.7	14.3	16.8
Latvia	12.8	29.6	19.3	17.4
Kirgizstan	11.4	22.9	13.8	16.6
Tadzjikistan	10.7	18.5	10.5	14.7
Armenia	11.4	20.3	11.7	15.7
Turkmenistan	10.6	17.8	10.0	13.9
Estonia	12.1	26.1	16.8	15.8

	Actual 1988	1993
Russia	58.0	25.5
Ukraine	79.0	57.5
Belarus	85.8	81.0
Uzbekistan	85.8	61.6
Kazakhstan	86.3	70.6
Georgia	86.5	51.6
Azerbaidzjan	85.6	64.8
Lithuania	86.8	63.3
Moldova	87.8	78.2
Latvia	86.7	60.7
Kirgizstan	86.8	74.7
Tadzjikistan	86.2	33.1
Armenia	89.1	56.6
Turkmenistan	89.0	57.8
Estonia	85.0	38.2

Sources. Van Selm and Wagener (1993: 28) for 1988, actual; Michalopoulos and Tarr (1994: 2–4) for 1993, actual; and calculations using the equations obtained by van Selm, Bergstrand, Wang and Winters, and Linneman. These equations were:

van Selm: $\ln(\text{trade}_{ij}) = 4.28 + 0.86 \ln(\text{GNP}_i \times \text{GNP}_j) - 0.58 \ln(\text{distance})$;
Bergstrand: $\ln(\text{trade}_{ij}) = 0.56 + 0.84 \ln(\text{GNP}_i) + 0.69 \ln(\text{GNP}_j) - 0.72 \ln(\text{distance}) + 0.74 \text{ dum(border)}$;
Wang and Winters: $\ln(\text{trade}_{ij}) = -12.49 + 1.17 \ln(\text{GNP}_i) - 0.38 \ln(\text{population}_i) + 1.02 \ln(\text{GNP}_j) - 0.22 \ln(\text{population}_j) - 0.75 \ln(\text{distance}) + 0.78 \text{ dum(border)}$;
Linneman: $\ln(\text{trade}_{ij}) = 0.13 + 0.99 \ln(\text{GNP}_i) - 0.20 \ln(\text{population}_i) + 0.85 \ln(\text{GNP}_j) - 0.15 \ln(\text{population}_j) - 0.81 \ln(\text{distance})$.

(the one using the Bergstrand equation) only 26 per cent of foreign trade can be expected to take place with other Soviet republics in the future. The main part of this trade reorientation had already materialised by 1993: data by Michalopoulos and Tarr (1994: 6) indicate that only 38.2 per cent of external Estonian trade was conducted with other Newly Independent States in 1993. The same is true for Russia: internal trade in 1988 was 58.0 per cent of total trade; in 1993, this share had already declined to 25.5 per cent, which is not so far off the 18.2 per cent predicted using the Bergstrand equation. In the last column of Table 5.3, we present the 1993 percentages of intra-USSR trade as derived from the data set in Michalopoulos and Tarr (1994: 2–4).

In Table 5.4, we present the distribution of trade over the four partner areas as obtained using the Bergstrand coefficients. As expected on account of both its proximity and its size, the EU stands out as an important future trade partner. The proximity of Central Asia to China and Japan matters.

This 'gravity' outcome is compatible with modern economic theorising on international trade. Very briefly, these ideas can be summarised as follows. A distinction is made between inter-industry trade and intra-industry trade, and between developed

Table 5.4 Predicted trade distribution (percentages)

	Former USSR	Japan+	China	EU+	USA+
Russia	18.2	22.1	5.4	38.9	15.3
Ukraine	29.5	9.4	2.3	43.7	15.1
Belarus	36.1	8.5	2.0	39.7	13.7
Uzbekistan	19.8	20.7	5.4	34.4	19.7
Kazakhstan	21.4	18.9	10.4	31.4	17.9
Georgia	26.0	13.2	3.1	39.8	17.9
Azerbaidzjan	23.4	13.7	3.2	41.2	18.6
Lithuania	32.2	8.4	1.9	43.3	14.2
Moldova	23.7	10.2	2.4	47.4	16.4
Latvia	29.6	8.7	2.0	44.9	14.8
Kirgizstan	22.9	18.5	10.0	30.9	17.7
Tadzjikistan	18.5	19.6	10.6	32.7	18.7
Armenia	20.3	14.2	3.4	42.9	19.3
Turkmenistan	17.8	21.2	5.5	35.4	20.2
Estonia	26.1	9.1	2.0	47.2	15.5

Sources: Author's calculations using Bergstrand's equation
Japan+ = Japan and South Korea; USA+ = USA and Canada; EU+ includes Sweden and Switzerland.

and developing countries. Intra-industry trade, based on scale economies, takes place among the developed economies; inter-industry trade, based on comparative advantage, is conducted between developed economies on the one hand and developing economies on the other. Little trade is expected, however, among the developing economies. The typical textbook illustration for this theory is Latin America, where countries trade much more with developed economies than among each other. Similarly, there might be few potential gains from trade among the developing republics of the former USSR.

IMPLICATIONS FOR POTENTIAL 'FORMER SOVIET' INSTITUTIONS

The intensity of trade relations is an important indicator of the potential success of Customs Unions and Monetary Unions. This variable features in Customs Union analysis on the cost side and Monetary Union analysis on the benefit side (see Chapter 6).

A country that enters in a Customs Union should avoid 'trade diversion' as much as possible. That is, buying products in the partner country that could be bought more cheaply in third counties is welfare reducing. The 'trade diversion' risk is minimised if the integration partners of the new member are important 'natural' trade partners. From the percentages in Table 5.3, we see that much less than half of total trade is carried out with other former Soviet republics in a 'natural' situation. Hence, the risk of 'trade diversion ' is substantial for a former Soviet Customs Union.

Trade intensity is an important indicator of the potential benefits of Monetary Union. These benefits stem from a reduction in transaction costs, risk and uncertainty. The lower the trade inten-sity of the potential partners, the lower these benefits are. Table 5.3 indicates that such benefits might be low in the case of the former Soviet Union.

An interesting question is whether the inverse relation can also be found empirically. Can the results obtained in gravity analysis be improved by inclusion of an 'economic integration' dummy? Dif-ferent empirical results have been found regarding this. Van Ber-geyk and Oldersma (1990: 602) did not find a significant correlation coefficient for membership of trade or customs unions, whereas Vjugin and Vavilov (1992) did find a significant correlation for EFTA membership. In recent gravity studies of trade among market economies, Baldwin (1994: 88) found a significant effect for membership of the 'European Economic Area' (i.e. for membership of either the EU or EFTA) from 1979 to 1988, and Eichengreen (1993b: 103) found a significant effect for the membership of the European Payments Union in the 1950s. More research is needed to give a more definitive answer to the question of what are the effects of membership of different forms of economic unions on trade intensities.

CONCLUSION

The gravity model functions extremely well when applied to the former Soviet Union. The pattern of interrepublican exchange fits 'gravity' extraordinarily well. The explanation of this phenomenon can be found in Soviet central planning. Stochastic influences, historical ties and cultural differences play a much more significant role in trade between market economies than in goods exchange between the regions of a planned economy. Here we may at last have found one aspect of where the economic rationality of planning is higher than that of the market.

On the basis of the estimated coefficients, we can predict a large trade reorientation. Goods exchange used to be concentrated within the Soviet Union, but can be expected to concentrate on the EU in the near future, especially in the case of the republics located in the west of the former USSR. The reorientation of trade is so extensive as to put the usefulness of a former Soviet monetary or customs area into doubt. Monetary and Customs Unions are the subject of the next chapter in this book.

6

THE SOVIET UNION AS A CUSTOMS AND MONETARY UNION

This chapter analyses which indicators a country can use to choose both the right partners to integrate with and the right form of integration (Monetary Union, Customs Union, or both) with these partners. The relevant variables turn out to be openness, level of development, factor mobility and federal budget redistribution. The results are applied to assess the economic rationality of the processes of integration and disintegration in Europe. Both the Euro's and the rouble's desirability as a shared currency can be questioned on account of limited factor mobility and budget redistributive capacities. A former Soviet Customs Union might very well be 'trade diverting', but can prove helpful as an instrument of development policy.

INTRODUCTION

Discussing the mixed blessings of economic integration has a long history in economic literature. Mr Methuen's Treaty of 1703, which admitted Portuguese wines into Great Britain on preferential terms in return for the removal of a prohibition on British woollen exports to Portugal, was hailed for 'gaining Great Britain above a Million a Year'. Adam Smith, however, called the treaty 'evidently disadvantageous to Great Britain', on account of what would be called 'trade diversion' today (Smith 1976: 546–7). Recent events in both Eastern Europe (the disintegration of the Soviet Union, Yugoslavia, Czechoslovakia and the collapse of the Council of Mutual Economic Assistance) and Western Europe (the Maastricht decisions on a common European currency), as well as in North America (the NAFTA agreement), have provided a new impetus for the development of economic integration theory. This chapter presents an overview of both old and new ideas, identifies the relevant success indicators of economic integration and presents case studies of the EU and the former USSR.

The literature of economic integration theory concentrates on two main forms: Customs Unions and Monetary Unions.[1] They can be defined as a group of geographical entities that have agreed both to abolish internal barriers to trade and to adopt common external tariffs in the case of the former and a common currency in the case of the latter.[2] In handbooks on economic integration, Monetary Union is often presented as a higher form of economic integration than Customs Union, sometimes implying that it can be achieved only at a later stage in the process of convergence of the participating members. As a consequence, a Monetary Union is defined to contain a Customs Union. In principle, however, the two concepts can very well be separated, and we shall do so in this chapter. Customs Union and Monetary Union theory are dealt with in the next two sections respectively. The subsequent section combines the results obtained, and applies them to test the economic rationality of the processes of integration and disintegration in Europe. The final section concludes.

CUSTOMS UNIONS THEORY

Why do countries join Customs Unions? In order to be able to provide an answer to this question, it should be split in two: 1 why do countries liberalise their trade with *some* other countries; and 2 why do they not liberalise their trade with *all* other countries? The textbook answer to the first question is that by joining a Customs Union and hence freeing mutual trade, economic gain can possibly be derived from a more efficient allocation of resources. Specialisation according to comparative advantage and increased output arising from better exploitation of scale economies are possible. Also, the partners might profit from forced changes in X-efficiency arising from increased competition within the group. However, all these are arguments in favour of worldwide free trade, not in favour of bilateral free trade. Yet, Customs Unions are an important fact of life. By what forces can their existence be explained?

Political economy arguments have been applied to answer this question. For example, Hirschman (1980) suggested that Customs Unions are formed because of the political support from a small group of people who gain from a Customs Union; that is, the people who benefit from 'trade diversion'. If country A joins country B in a Customs Union, exporters in B obtain a competitive advantage on A's market over exporters in C that also try to sell their goods in A. Similarly, a group of exporters from A obtains a competitive advantage on B's market. If A and B buy each other's products even though C offers the same products at a lower price, then total welfare in both A and B is reduced. The price is paid by the consumers in the two countries. Unfortunately, their losses are dispersed over a multitude of subjects, which is difficult to organise politically. In this interpretation, Customs Unions are formed for the wrong reason.

An alternative 'right reason' explanation for the existence of Customs Unions can be found in the application of dynamic instead of static arguments. Free trade is beneficial to all parties concerned in static terms.[3] In a dynamic setting, however, free trade reinforces existing divisions of labour. It is a notable fact that in world history, the leading economy has often promoted free trade (Holland in the seventeenth century, Great Britain in the nineteenth and the USA in the twentieth). Customs Unions can be used as a protective device for promoting infant industries, as was already noted by Friedrich List.[4] More recently, arguments against free trade employing dynamic analysis have been formulated by Krugman (1987). His idea of a strategic trade policy is directly relevant to Customs Union analysis. If international trade is not ruled by comparative advantage and factor endowments, but rather by increasing returns to scale, then 'whichever firm manages to establish itself in the industry will earn supernormal profits that will not be competed away' (Krugman 1987: 135). If A and B form a Customs Union, this might help firms in A and B to establish such a position.

Once worldwide free trade has been ruled out, the question becomes one of who, if anyone, to pick as an integration partner. This requires a comparison of the welfare effects of no economic integration versus biased integration, which is the field of Customs Union analysis. Usually, Viner's classic 1950 work is taken as its starting point. According to Viner (1950: 44 ff.), the welfare effects of a Customs Union can be split into 'trade creation' and 'trade diversion'. Viewed from the perspective of country A, benefits from economic integration, 'trade creation', arise because production that formerly took place in A now takes place in partner country B. The welfare-reducing 'trade diversion' effect stems from imports that used to come from a third country C and that now come from B. The relative magnitude of these effects depends on a number of variables, such as the elasticities of the demand and supply schedules and the magnitude of the difference between domestic and foreign prices. The total welfare effect for country A can be obtained by subtracting trade diversion from trade creation.

Of course, the result thus obtained hinges on a long list of assumptions. Not surprisingly, changing the assumptions also changes the results. In this way, many other effects have been 'discovered', e.g. trade suppression (Robson 1980: 36), trade modification (Ethier 1985: 478) and trade destruction (Holzman 1987: 171).

More fundamentally, the results become ambiguous if Viner's one-good partial equilibrium analysis is extended to a two-goods general equilibrium analysis. Lipsey (1970: chapter 4) showed that a Customs Union can increase welfare without any 'trade creation' as defined above. For this reason, Customs Union theory has been dubbed 'one of the more disappointing branches of postwar economics' (Pomfret 1986) and the terms 'trade creation' and 'trade diversion' have been called inadequate and even blamed for retarding progress in Customs Union analysis for forty years (Kowalczyk 1990). Kowalczyk has proposed using the concepts of 'terms of trade effect' and 'volume of trade effect' instead. Using this terminology, he gives a rigorous proof of Lipsey's (1970: 56) proposition that

> a Customs Union is more likely to raise welfare, *given the total volume of imports of the country*, the larger is the proportion of these imports obtained from the country's union partners and the less is the proportion devoted to imports from the outside world.

> (emphasis by Lipsey)

Lipsey's proposition is intuitively appealing. It is clear that the negative effects stemming from a switch in trade from buying something from a third party to buying something from the partner country should be avoided as much as possible, irrespective of whether this effect is called 'trade diversion' or 'terms of trade effect'. From this proposition, an operational variable can be derived that can be used to decide who is a suitable partner. A partner or a group of partners that accounts for an important part of foreign trade should be selected.[5]

Also, it seems obvious that whether we talk about 'volume of trade effect' or 'trade creation effect', benefits should be derived somehow from a different division of labour between the two partners concerned. Trade creation, i.e. a shift from domestic production to foreign production, cannot exist if no products are produced in both countries. If one is a producer of raw materials and the other produces advanced industrial products, then the division of labour will probably hardly be altered by the Customs Union. The link that has often been found in empirical studies between international economic integration and intra-industry trade is not a coincidence (Greenaway 1989). The two partners involved should have some activities in common that allow for an increase in specialisation (Pelkmans 1984: 14; Robson 1980: 17). From this we derive a second operational variable: countries that join a Customs Union should have comparable levels of development.

To recapitulate, manifold as its caveats may be, Customs Union analysis renders two determinants that can be operationalised empirically, as partners in a Customs Union choose those who (1) are important trading partners already (so that the risk of trade diversion is minimised) and (2) have a comparable level of development (so that the possibilities for trade creation are maximised). These findings are reaffirmed by real world experience. The EU has been a success because intra-EU trade is an important part of total trade for the participating member states, and because levels of development are comparable, especially among the original six (see Tables 6.2 and 6.3 below). Conversely, attempts to create trading blocs in Latin America and Africa failed on account of too limited potential for internal trade (Foroutan 1993: 253; Nogués and Quintanilla 1993: 298) and too widely diverging levels of development (Foroutan 1993: 257; Nogués and Quintanilla 1993: 296).

MONETARY UNIONS

The Maastricht decisions on a single European currency, envisaged for 1999, have put the economics of Monetary Unions in the spotlight. As in the case of a Customs Union, the decision whether or not to join a currency area depends on an assessment of the costs and benefits involved. The benefits of a Monetary Union lie in the reduction of risks and transaction costs. In the EU, a round trip of an amount of money among the twelve member states would produce a 50 per cent loss on the original sum (CEC 1990a: 66). Probably more important is the reduction of risk and uncertainties. In a world of risk-averse agents, moving to a single currency is like providing free and perfect foreign exchange hedging to all. Because losses stemming from a devaluation are ruled out once a Monetary Union is created, capital mobility (both portfolio investment and foreign direct investment) is increased, leading to potential welfare improvements. Also, wrong incentives stemming from exchange rate over- or undervaluation can be avoided. Finally, 'credibility' arguments in favour of a Monetary Union have recently been advanced. It has been argued that, for example, by adopting the Euro a country like Italy can import 'Bundesbank' reliability and hence price stability. However, it is doubtful whether this really should be counted on the plus side of the ledger. Italy could also create its own Bundesbank (Bean 1992: 41).

The benefits of a Monetary Union can be linked to the intensity of mutual trade. Decreasing uncertainty and a reduction in transaction costs are not very helpful if there is no trade with the country considered anyway. The benefits of a Monetary Union increase with openness towards the potential partner.

On the cost side of Monetary Unions, a distinction should be made between arguments that relate to economic 'fundamentals' and arguments related to 'shock adjustment'. Starting with the former, countries that have widely diverging levels of development might incur high costs when entering a Monetary Union because they have different inflation preferences. Originally, this argument was used in the context of a Phillips curve (Fleming, reproduced in El-Agraa 1990: 102). Different countries might opt for a different choice in the tradeoff between unemployment and inflation. This would create a need for nominal exchange rate adjustment at regular time intervals. However, this argument vanishes if the faith in a stable Phillips curve disappears. Alternatively, countries might have different inflation preferences because the optimal level of monetary financing of the government budget may diverge. Especially for developing countries, this level may be substantial, because of the difficulties encountered in levying taxes on the population. A developed economy would normally prefer to have income and value-added taxes in combination with price stability. Hence, the costs of a common currency are related to the level of development of the countries that consider a monetary union.

Also, 'real' arguments have been put forward (Melitz 1991). In the long run, real interest rates are determined by time preference and capital productivity. In turn, time preference is determined by such factors as a country's age structure and 'national character'. Countries with different attitudes with respect to time should have different real interest rates. The argument is that the option of having different real interest rates is lost if a common currency is adopted. However, the possibility of having different real interest rates across countries is lost not because of a single currency, but rather because of a single market. A common real interest rate is caused by capital mobility, not by a common currency. Only in so far as a common currency increases capital mobility can this effect be blamed on the common currency.

In the 'shock adjustment' line of reasoning, the exchange rate is lost as an instrument of economic policy if a common currency is formed. The basic idea is that an adjustment mechanism is needed to redress the balance if two countries that are united in a common currency area suffer from an asymmetric demand or supply shock, giving rise to a balance of payments inequilibrium and diverging patterns of economic performance. Three questions are relevant in this context:

1 do the parties involved suffer from asymmetric shocks;
2 is the exchange rate an appropriate tool for adjustment; and
3 is an alternative tool available?

On the first question, the more 'similar' the two countries involved, the less need there is for exchange rate adjustment. In his classic 1961 article on optimum currency areas, Mundell (1961: 659) criticised the Canadian experiment with a flexible exchange rate because of the similarity between the economies of the USA and Canada. In the next section below, we use the level of development as a rough approximation of the similarity between countries or regions. Yet, even if economies have a similar level of development, asymmetric shocks will remain, because countries or regions specialise in different economic sectors. In an attempt to quantify the correlation of shocks between regions in the USA, and between member states of the European Community, Bayoumi and

Eichengreen (1992) found that both demand and supply shocks are far from perfectly correlated.

On the second question, McKinnon, in his equally classic 1963 article, stressed the importance of openness. In his view, a Monetary Union is beneficial if there is a high degree of openness within the region and a low degree of openness between the area and the rest of the world. For, if a country is open, a change in the exchange rate does not improve the balance of trade as an exchange rate change increases the price of tradables relative to non-tradables, so that the production of tradables is stimulated and consumption shifts from tradables to non-tradables. Hence, on the cost side of Monetary Union analysis, openness is a relevant variable.

If the two partners suffer from asymmetric shocks, but decide to join in a Monetary Union anyway, the need for an alternative mechanism of adjustment arises. In Mundell's classical optimum currency area theory, labour mobility plays this role. The idea is that in case of an asymmetric shock, such as a shift in tastes from the production of region A to the production of region B, unemployment might result if prices and wages are slow to adjust and the exchange rate cannot be adjusted, unless labour is mobile and can move from region A to region B.

The importance of labour mobility as an adjustment mechanism is reinforced by recent empirical findings on shock adjustment in the US economy. Here we have a Monetary Union that suffers from asymmetric shocks, because the regional concentration of economic sectors in the USA is high. Blanchard and Katz (1992: 52) found that in the case of a negative demand shock, labour moves out of a US state. Even though wages decline, few jobs move in. This result surprised those who expected that capital mobility would be higher than labour mobility.[6] An explanation can be found in modern international trade theory, as de la Dehesa and Krugman (1992: 6) suggest. In a traditional neoclassical framework, one would expect capital to move to a region where labour is abundant and where wages are low. In a modern increasing returns to scale setting, however, capital moves to places where a certain amount of capital has settled already. This implies that if a region is hit by an asymmetric demand shock capital mobility increases the problem.

A second important adjustment mechanism found in the USA is fiscal redistribution. Sala-i-Martin and Sachs (1991: 18–19) explained the success of the USA as a Monetary Union by pointing out that 40 per cent of an initial demand shock is made up of automatic fiscal transfers.[7] Eichengreen (1991: 24) confirmed this result by showing that, apart from labour mobility, fiscal redistribution played an important role in dealing with an asymmetric shock to Michigan, caused by the second oil crisis. This mechanism of adjustment could be especially important in circumstances where labour mobility is a less desirable mechanism for adjustment. In the German monetary unification, for example, wages in the Eastern parts were set relatively close to wage levels in the Western *Länder* precisely with the aim of restricting migration flows. Instead, the adjustment mechanism that was used in Germany was a large-scale fiscal transfer (de Grauwe 1992).

The case for a substantial union budget with redistribution capacities in a Monetary Union is strengthened by the fact that the room for an independent fiscal policy at the subfederal level decreases as one enters a Monetary Union.[8] In the Maastricht Treaty, explicit rules have even been set for the members' budget deficits. The economic rationality of these rules has been debated vehemently (see e.g. Buiter *et al.* 1993). However, even if no rules are explicitly formulated, the degrees of freedom decline. For example, member states cannot afford to raise significantly higher taxes than other member states, because of possible tax evasion of productive factors.

THEORY APPLIED TO THE EU AND THE FORMER USSR

We can summarise the results with respect to Customs Unions and Monetary Unions as follows. Openness increases the benefits and reduces the costs of Monetary Union. Moreover, the costs of a Monetary Union are lower if the levels of development of the two partners are more similar. Here we rediscover the same two determinants that we found in the case of a Customs Union. If the mutual exchange of goods is high and if the levels of development are similar, both a Customs Union and a Monetary Union would probably be a success from an economic point of view. However, in the case of a Monetary Union more variables (factor mobility and budget redistributive capacities) are relevant. This could serve as an economic explanation for the fact that Monetary Unions are often Customs Unions as well. The reverse statement does not hold. The ideas discussed in this chapter are presented in a comprehensive form in Table 6.1. In this table the institutional setting is expressed horizontally and the success indicators vertically. The relevant paradigms have been given a (+) sign if they relate to the benefit side of union and a (−) sign if they are connected to the cost side.

It is important to differentiate between *ex ante* and *ex post* success requirements. Openness should be high *before* the two partners form a Customs Union. Once a Customs Union is formed, the level of goods exchange may be quite high, but this may be trade of the 'trade-diverting' type. Hence, high openness is an *ex ante* requirement.

As regards the level of development, the question of *ex ante* versus *ex post* can be converted in the convergence–divergence debate. If economic integration leads to economic convergence, then the disadvantages that are connected to an integration partner with a different level of development will disappear over time. It is by no means sure that economic integration does lead to economic convergence, however. On the contrary, recent economic models predict higher interregional inequalities over time, on account of scale economies (see e.g. Krugman 1991). A similar level of development is an *ex ante* requirement only if we assume that there is no or slow convergence.

High factor mobility in the case of a Monetary Union is in principle an *ex post* requirement. Even if factor mobility is not very high, if *by the creation of a Monetary Union* it is made very high, then there is no problem. Indeed, the creation of a common currency can be expected to raise the level of capital mobility

Table 6.1 Economic integration theory

	Customs Unions	Monetary Unions
Openness	Trade diversion (−)	Transaction costs and/ or uncertainty reduction (+) Shock absorption (−)
Level of development	Trade creation (+)	Inflation tax (−) Shock absorption (−)
Factor mobility and/or budget redistributive capacities		Shock absorption (−)

significantly. However, as we have seen, capital mobility is an unreliable mechanism of adjustment. It seems unlikely that the creation of a common currency would have an important bearing on labour mobility. Hence, even though strictly speaking the requirement that labour mobility be high is an *ex post* requirement, in practice the level of *ex ante* labour mobility can be taken as a good proxy.

Let us now try to apply the results obtained to EU monetary integration. The debate over whether or not the EU is an optimum currency area is not new. In the 1950s, Meade (1957: 385–6) considered labour mobility too low in Europe. But according to Scitovsky (1958: chapter 2) something should and could be done about that. Evidently, they applied Mundell-type arguments *avant la lettre*. On the benefit side of Monetary Union, the CEC (1990a: 21, 63) estimated the benefits from a reduction in transaction costs to some 0.5 per cent of Community GNP and the benefits from the reduction of risk and uncertainty to 5–10 per cent of European GNP. An impression of the distribution of these gains from Monetary Union over the member states can be obtained via EU openness ratios. These were presented in Table 4.2. The ratios suggest that the benefits related to the creation of a single currency are not equally distributed. The reduction in transaction costs and uncertainty is most important for Ireland, Belgium, Portugal and the Netherlands. These countries have high internal EU openness, when expressed both as a percentage of GNP and relative to extra-EU openness.

Openness also reduces the costs of Monetary Union. However, on the cost side more factors are relevant. Differences in the level of development (see Table 6.2) indicate that countries might have different preferences with respect to the use of the inflation tax and that they might be susceptible to asymmetric shocks. The former argument is irrelevant in Western Europe, because even the least developed countries make little use of the inflation tax, so that there is no real problem here (CEC 1990a: 121). The latter argument is more important in the discussion about the costs of a common currency for the EU member states. Portugal, Greece, Spain and Ireland have all the characteristics of countries in a lower stage of their economic development: lower GNP per capita, a larger share of output in agriculture, and a lower share in services. If, for example, a worldwide slump in agriculture were to occur, these countries would be hit harder than the more developed

Table 6.2 EU levels of development

Country	GDP/capita (current US$)	Economic structure (% in economy)		
		Agriculture	Industry	Services
Belgium	15,180	2.0	31.1	66.9
Denmark	20,926	4.2	28.1	67.7
Germany	19,581	1.5	39.9	58.6
Greece	5,244	15.8	28.3	55.9
Spain	8,722	5.1	37.4	57.5
France	17,002	3.5	30.6	65.9
Ireland	9,182	9.7	36.8	53.5
Italy	14,430	3.7	34.3	62.0
Luxemburg	17,592	2.1	32.6	65.3
Netherlands	15,461	4.3	32.5	63.2
Portugal	4,264	6.3	38.0	55.7
United Kingdom	14,413	1.0	35.5	63.5
EU		3.0	35.4	61.6

Sources: Eurostat (1990: 43) for economic structure; OECD Economic Survey (any issue) for GDP per capita at current prices. Data for 1988

group. A devaluation might be the appropriate response, but this would be impossible once there is a single European currency.[9]

Asymmetric shocks would not pose a problem if an alternative for the exchange rate as a mechanism for adjustment existed. But such an alternative is absent in the EU. Budget redistribution among member states is low. The present EU budget (some 1 per cent of EU GNP) is not capable of fulfilling a significant redistribution function. A simple calculation by Eichengreen (1990: 141) makes clear that if a US level of shock absorption via the budget is to be achieved, the EU budget needs significant enlargement. This conclusion is reinforced by empirical evidence on 1980 intra-EU transfers (Swann 1988: 77). For all member states except Ireland, net grants to or donations from other member states amounted to less than 1 per cent of GNP. Moreover, if the EU budget is to play a redistributive role, its principles should be changed fundamentally. At present, on the receipts side the EU budget system is regressive instead of progressive. The value-added tax (VAT) hits the poor more than proportionally, because a higher fraction of a low income is consumed, and VAT is a tax on consumption (de la Dehesa and Krugman 1992: 21). The main entry on the expenditure side, the Common Agricultural Policy, does not lead to rich-to-poor redistribution either.

Hence, factor mobility must carry the main part of the burden of adjustment if a common currency is introduced. It is doubtful if it can. West European labour mobility is low (CEC 1990a: 46). Conversely, capital mobility is both high and equality promoting (CEC 1990a: 160; de la Dehesa and Krugman 1992: 21). It remains to be seen, however, whether capital flows will continue to play this beneficial role. The American experience is not encouraging in this respect.

In conclusion, the economic success of a common currency in Western Europe is questionable. The central problem is that there is no well-developed mechanism that can take over the role of the exchange rate in the case of asymmetric shocks. Interestingly, the relative support for monetary unification in the different EU member states is to some extent reflected in the costs and benefits involved. The openness ratios indicate that two countries which showed little enthusiasm, Denmark and the UK, have little to gain from monetary unification. On the other hand, countries like Belgium and the Netherlands that have most to gain because of high openness have been highly supportive.

Beneficial or not, the Maastricht Treaty with its commitment to a common currency has been ratified by all member states now. The introduction of a unified currency is far from certain, however, as the treaty has made its introduction contingent on a number of stringent criteria. One of these criteria is that countries must stick to stable exchange rates, i.e. within their normal EMS fluctuation bands, for two years preceding entry. With the demise and redefinition of the EMS, it is unclear how this criterion is to be interpreted. The same goes for the fiscal criteria in the Maastricht Treaty. Regarding the fact that very few members meet these criteria, they must be either neglected or renegotiated.[10] The monetary future of Western Europe is still open.

Next, let us turn to the East. Recent events in Europe make it clear that creating new currencies is easier than abandoning old ones. Western Europe is moving only slowly, dropping established currencies in favour of the Euro, whereas lats (Latvia), lits (Lithuania), leis (Moldova) and laris (Georgia) have been introduced in the Newly Independent States. Political factors played an important role in the decision to leave the rouble zone. Together with the flag and the national anthem, the currency is one of the main symbols of state, and such symbols are especially important for new states trying to put themselves on the world map. The question we address here is whether the decision to introduce a national currency can also be justified from an economic point of view.

On the cost side of the rouble as a common currency for the former Soviet republics, a problem corresponding to that in the EU exists. There is no alternative adjustment mechanism that can replace the exchange rate. The federal Soviet budget has disappeared, and interrepublican redistribution cannot be expected to continue much longer (van Selm and Dölle 1993; see Chapter 8). On top of this, free mobility of labour is very unlikely to say the least. Present ethnic tensions do not allow for that. Capital mobility cannot be expected to come to the rescue either, because capital markets are virtually non-existent in the former Soviet Union. If the exchange rate is given up as a mechanism for adjustment, neither the budget nor factor mobility can be used as a substitute.

The data presented in Table 6.3 indicate that asymmetric shocks are very likely in the former Soviet Union. The levels of development differ widely. Moreover, the inflation tax argument is relevant in this case. At present all the former Soviet republics are trying to set up new tax systems. Under Communism, the state's receipts relied heavily on profit taxes and turnover taxes. In a market setting, personal income tax and value-added tax are more important. The introduction of these new tax systems is likely to be much easier in the more developed republics. Hence, especially during the period of transition to a new tax system, the less developed republics will probably have to rely much more on inflation tax than the more developed republics.

With respect to the benefits of a common rouble, data on openness in Table 4.1 show that the intra-Union ratio and the ratio of intra- to extra-Union trade found here are considerably higher than in the case of the EU. However, here we clearly have an *ex ante* problem. For the peripheral republics, extra-USSR trade was seriously hampered by the central foreign trade monopoly. Today, the level of goods exchange among the republics is decreasing at a rapid pace. Gravity models can be used to find more 'natural' levels of intra-FSU and extra-FSU trade. This was done in Chapter 5.

In the short run, however, goods exchange between the former Soviet republics remains substantial, and this might be an argument for keeping the rouble for a certain transition period. Up until April 1992, this was the reason why the IMF advised former Soviet

Table 6.3 USSR levels of development

	GNP/capita USSR=100	Economic structure (% in economy)				
		agriculture	industry	construction	transport	other
Russia	115.8	19.9	42.2	12.7	6.9	18.3
Ukraine	92.9	30.3	41.3	9.7	6.0	19.4
Belarus	116.6	29.3	44.0	11.8	5.1	9.8
Uzbekistan	51.1	44.0	23.8	14.9	5.7	11.4
Kazakhstan	71.5	39.9	27.6	15.3	9.3	7.9
Georgia	91.9	37.2	35.0	11.0	4.9	11.9
Azerbaidzjan	84.6	37.6	34.8	11.7	5.2	10.8
Lithuania	109.9	33.4	34.1	13.4	5.9	13.3
Moldova	85.1	41.7	34.4	9.0	4.8	10.1
Latvia	124.2	21.8	51.2	8.1	7.5	11.3
Kirgizstan	56.3	43.1	31.8	11.9	3.8	9.2
Tadzjikistan	45.8	38.3	28.6	14.7	4.2	14.3
Armenia	82.8	17.3	45.4	25.4	4.1	7.8
Turkmenistan	67.1	47.9	15.7	17.9	8.5	10.1
Estonia	121.6	20.3	50.5	10.5	7.2	11.5

Sources: GNP per capita data for 1988 reproduced from Table 3.6; World Bank (1992: 6–7) for economic structure (data for 1990)

republics to stick to the rouble.[11] However, the disadvantage of keeping the rouble as a common currency in the short run was the creation of a free rider problem. With many fiscal authorities sharing a common currency, the incentives to create money are strong, because the benefits of increased spending accrue only to the spending republic, whereas the costs (increased inflation) are spread over the whole area. This arrangement proved very conducive to inflation in 1991, with the Russian government as the biggest spender; the fiscal deficit of Russia in 1991 was 20 per cent of Russian GNP! Ukraine, with a deficit of 14.4 per cent of its GNP, was a good second. Many of the other republics seemed not to understand the game and ran a fiscal surplus (IMF 1992: 39). When the Soviet Union ceased to exist, the Russian government made stabilisation a primary economic goal, and saw its attempts to stabilise frustrated by inflationary policies in the other republics. Attempts are now being made to stop the flow of peripheral roubles to Russia. Republican account roubles were made inconvertible to Russian account roubles in July 1992. One year later, central bank president Gerashchenko defended his monetary reform as an attempt to do the same for cash roubles. Indeed, for Georgia, Turkmenistan, Azerbaidzjan and Moldova, the events of July 1993 were reason to leave or speed up leaving the rouble zone (Ukraine, Estonia, Latvia, Lithuania, Belarus and Kirgizstan had already left the rouble zone). The remaining republics followed in November 1993, with the exception of only Tadzjikistan which introduced its own currency as late as March 1995. Table 6.4 presents the exchange rates of the currencies in the Newly Independent States as of 3 November 1995.

What about the prospects for a Customs Union covering the area of the former USSR? As we have seen, a Customs Union is likely to be successful if the partners are 'natural' trading partners and if the economies have a similar level of development. Again, high as the openness ratios may have been under Soviet rule (Table 4.1), it remains to be seen whether there is much room for trade between former Soviet republics in the future. If extra-FSU trade becomes far more important than intra-FSU trade, in line with the predictions of Chapter 5, the danger of trade diversion is imminent. Also, differences in the level of development are quite substantial (Table 6.3), and hence possibilities for trade creation might

Table 6.4 The new currencies

	Date of own currency introduction	Cash market exchange rate
Ukrainian karbovanets	November 1992	40,000.0
Belarussian rouble	January 1993	2,550.0
Uzbekistan sum	November 1993	6.02
Kazakhstan tenge	November 1993	12.3
Georgian lari	August 1993	0.4
Azerbaidzjan manat	January 1994	860.0
Lithuanian lit	October 1992	0.82
Moldovan lei	July 1993	1.1
Latvian lat	June 1992	0.11
Kirgizstan som	May 1993	2.38
Tadzjikistan rouble	March 1995	n/a
Armenian dram	November 1993	86.0
Turkmenistan manat	November 1993	165.0
Estonian crown	June 1992	2.41

Sources: Centre for Economic Reforms (1994, no.2: 30; 1995, no.1: 34) for dates of currency introduction and (1995, no.3: 36) for exchange rates. Exchange rates per 1,000 Russian roubles on 3 November 1995

be limited. The economic success of a former Soviet customs area is far from evident.

The case for a Customs Union among the states of the former Soviet Union can be made stronger if it is interpreted in a dynamic sense. This 'Listian' argument was recently repeated by Dornbusch (1992: 419), who stated that 'freeing regional trade and discriminating somewhat in favour of the region is a good development policy'.[12]

CONCLUSION

In this chapter we derived four success indicators from Customs Union and Monetary Union theory. Surprisingly, we found that although the nature of the two bodies of theory is quite different, the relevant variables overlap. Higher openness among potential integration partners increases the benefits of a Monetary Union and decreases the costs of a Customs Union. Conversely, more similarity in levels of development increases the benefits of a Customs Union and reduces the costs of a Monetary Union. Two additional variables, factor mobility and federal budget redistribution, are relevant in Monetary Union analysis. The higher factor mobility and budget redistribution, the lower the costs of a Monetary Union.

We used this outcome to assess the economic rationality of current processes of integration and disintegration in Europe. On account of the limited labour mobility and redistribution capacities of the budget in the EU, monetary unification of the EU may be costly. Private capital flows will have to accommodate asymmetric shocks. Openness ratios indicate that the benefits of monetary unification are unequally distributed. Small countries like Belgium and the Netherlands have most to gain from it.

In the former USSR, future prospects for budget redistribution and factor mobility are even gloomier. This implies that the decision of the majority of the republics to introduce their own currencies might be not only beneficial in the short run (because it avoids sharing a common currency with a number of independent fiscal authorities), but also rational from a long-term economic point of view. High openness among the Newly Independent States indicates that important benefits from a common currency exist, but this interrepublican trade is nosediving now and it remains to be seen at what level it stabilises. The preconditions for a successful Customs Union are less demanding. A Customs Union might be a useful tool of development policy in the former Soviet area.

In the absence of a Monetary Union, a Payments Union could be considered as an alternative. This is the topic of the next chapter.

7

THE SOVIET UNION AS A PAYMENTS UNION

INTRODUCTION

Within the last few years, a number of articles have appeared addressing the possible merits of a Payments Union in the East. This chapter summarises this literature; it is interesting to analyse how well-known economists disagree and argue. We make clear that in the final analysis it is the degree of one's faith in the workings of the free market that determines one's position.

In the second part of this chapter, we follow the attempts to create a Payments Union in the CIS. It is the proponents of the idea that have advised the ex-Soviet governments on the matter over the past two years, and they have nudged the Newly Independent States towards the creation of a Payments Union. In the fourth section, we discuss the role and the position of the key players in this process of institution building: the AGIR group, the IMF, and the central banks of the Newly Independent States. We start by discussing the pros and cons of a Payments Union for the former Soviet Union in theory in the next two sections.

THE EUROPEAN PAYMENTS UNION EXPERIENCE, 1950–8

The precedent for a potential 'Eastern Payments Union' is the European Payments Union (EPU), a payments mechanism that functioned in Western Europe from 1950 to 1958. As this is the only successful example in world history of something called a 'Payments Union', the obvious way to define a 'Payments Union' would be to extract the essential elements of this historical episode and call that a 'Payments Union'. This is where the debate starts, because opinions differ on what the EPU was and whether it was a good thing or not. With respect to the term Payments Union, East European scholars, however, think first of CMEA. There is little disagreement on what CMEA was and, since this was a much less successful example of a Payments Union, there is a fair consensus in the East that CMEA has not been a good thing at all.

The standard description and assessment of the EPU runs as follows. After the Second World War the countries of Western Europe conducted their trade along the lines set out in some 200 bilateral treaties. Because of the inconvertibility of their currencies, they had to balance trade bilaterally instead of multilaterally. This reduced the amount of trade among them. The obvious solution to this problem, i.e. the reintroduction of convertibility, was impossible at the time, as is illustrated by the attempt of the UK to make sterling convertible to dollars in 1947. 'Although supported by credit lines of unprecedented magnitude, about 5 billion dollars, the UK authorities had to suspend convertibility after only seven weeks' (Gros and Thygesen 1992: 5). As an alternative, the EPU was introduced. The EPU facilitated trade among West European countries by supplying procedures for resolving trade imbalances via clearing, credit and settlement in gold and dollars. According to Dornbusch (1993: 95), the entire history of the EPU can be summarised by the data presented in Table 7.1.

Most important in reducing imbalances was multilateral clearing. If A owes B, B owes C, and C owes A, and the amount is the same in all cases, say 100 dollars, then these accounts can be settled without using any dollars. All that is needed for this is an institution that monitors the positions and clears them. In the EPU, this role was fulfilled by the Bank for International Settlements.

The second important mechanism for settlement was credit. If A owes B, a possible way of dealing with the unsettled account is to

Table 7.1 The European Payments Union, 1950–8 (billion US$)

Total bilateral positions	46.4
Multilateral compensation	20.0
Compensation through time	12.6
Gold and dollars	10.7
Special settlements	0.5
Credit balance outstanding	2.7

Source: Dornbusch (1993: 96)

leave it for some time and to hope that at some point in the future A sells more to B than vice versa, so that 'compensation through time' can take place. The credit mechanism in the EPU was linked to the rules for settlement in gold and dollars, which was the third important element in settlement (see Table 7.1). The positions of creditors and debtors in the system were not symmetrical. According to some, this asymmetry was an important reason for the success of the EPU (Gros and Thygesen 1992: 6). The asymmetry caused a need for some external finance, and this aid was delivered via the Marshall Plan, in the amount of US$ 350 million (Eichengreen 1993a: 333).

Thus, via clearing, credit and settlement in currencies and gold, the EPU promoted the expansion of trade among the countries of Western Europe. In 1958, these countries were ready for convertibility, and the EPU was no longer needed. As the episode of the EPU lies in between 1945, when West European states were impoverished and self-sufficient, and today's affluent and integrated West European society, the natural conclusion would be that the EPU was a success.

However, re-evaluations of the EPU claim that even better results might have been achieved if convertibility had been introduced right away. 'It took 13 years for Europe to reattain current account convertibility after the end of the war; it could have been done more rapidly, and at a lower economic cost' (Fischer 1993b: 349; see also Fischer 1993a). Even though convertibility and the EPU were not mutually exclusive, as the example of Switzerland proves (Williamson 1992: 30; Dornbusch 1993: 105), it does seem true that an important reason for having a convertible currency disappeared with the EPU, and that therefore the EPU might have slowed the introduction of convertible currencies in other European states.

The reason that is usually given to explain the impossibility of introducing convertibility is the 'structural balance of payments deficit'. That should account for the 1947 sterling débâcle in the UK. But would this deficit also have existed if the convertible sterling had been introduced at a lower exchange rate? A regression by Eichengreen (1993a: 320) shows that the answer to this question is probably no. Exports and imports in the immediate postwar period were considerably elastic, and a devaluation could have done the job. Eichengreen concludes that this can therefore not have been the reason for the EPU. But, as Fischer (1993b: 348) rightly points out, the important thing here is not whether elasticity coefficients were high at the time, but whether they were *believed* to be high at the time. Elasticity pessimism can very well explain the EPU.

Even if one believes that it is possible to create equilibrium at a lower exchange rate, this can be considered undesirable because one deems the exchange rate necessary for this as too low. In the EPU context, Eichengreen (1993a: 326–7) holds that in the EPU era the exchange rate of the European currencies *vis-à-vis* the USA was deliberately set above market clearing rates so as to improve the European terms of trade. Opting for convertibility would have reduced European incomes by 1–2 per cent. The same goal could have been achieved via tariff protection, but the rules of GATT were apparently stronger than those of the IMF (the IMF Articles of Agreement mandated convertibility after a transition period of three to five years). Indeed, relations between the EPU Management Board and the IMF were tense. Kaplan and Schleiminger (1989: 340) speak of 'mutual hostility'. 'Despite IMF insistence and some US urging, the Management Board refused to admit an IMF observer to its meetings until 1953' (Kaplan and Schleiminger 1989: 340).

The problem with this theory, however, is that not all European currencies were in fact overvalued with respect to the US dollar in the 1950s. If anything, the German Deutschmark was *under*valued to the dollar. Moreover, if the aim of the EPU was to increase the European terms of trade *vis-à-vis* the USA, then it seems as if not all EPU participants were aware of it. Already in June 1952, minister Aiken of Ireland proposed adding the USA and Canada to EPU membership (Kaplan and Schleiminger 1989: 168).

A debated point is whether less reserves are needed to run a Payments Union compared to introducing a convertible currency. Williamson (1992: 29) claims that

> it is often said that a clearing or Payments Union would be redundant if the republics introduce convertibility. This view is mistaken. In order to establish convertibility in the former Soviet republics without a Payments Union, it would be necessary to have reserves approaching five times as high as would be needed with such a union, given that about 80 per cent of trade is intratrade.

Dornbusch (1992: 101) is of the same opinion. But according to Eichengreen (1993a: 341), the need for reserves is exactly the same under the two systems, unless there is a credit facility, and a credit facility can exist only after stabilisation. This explains why the EPU was introduced in 1950, not in 1945. This also marks a difference with the situation in Eastern Europe in the early 1990s.

If convertibility with flexible exchange rates is introduced, there is no need for reserves at all. The example of Slovenia shows that this is a serious option (Mencinger 1994). As Slovenia had no reserves, the only available option was to introduce a currency at a freely floating exchange rate. Yet the Slovenian tolar proved to be surprisingly stable.

The success of the EPU was conditional upon the strong commitment of European governments to trade liberalisation, a precondition of the USA to grant aid under the Marshall Plan. Clearing was automatic and balancing a more or less *ex post* operation. Only in cases of extreme imbalances, as with Germany in the early 1950s, was the government allowed to intervene with import quotas and other protectionist measures (Kaplan and Schleiminger 1989: 110). The failure of CMEA was mainly due to the fact that, given the state monopoly of foreign trade, it could only be a clumsy clearing house of bilaterally trading countries. Balancing happened in principle *ex ante* and was by no means automatic.

Under a Payments Union regime all transactions within the union are geared through the clearing house. The necessary balancing of payments can be done by exchange rate policy, by export promotion which up to a limit (dumping) is considered market conforming, and by import control – a clearly protectionist measure. The foreign exchange markets are not operative and the banking sector plays only a passive role, if any at all. Yet gradual trade liberalisation is possible under such a regime. Monetary transactions with external partners have to be settled either bilaterally or in convertible currencies and, as a rule, are subjected to severe control. Hence the importance of the size of the union with respect to total foreign trade and hence the implicit tendency to discriminate against the external world.

The two systems – convertibility or a Payments Union – can also differ with respect to who decides what is traded. In a normal market economy, decentralised agents decide what is imported or exported. Under a Payments Union regime, governments can decide to accept only those transactions that they consider to be 'beneficial' (Fischer 1993b: 349). One reason for the success of the EPU was that, owing to their commitment to free trade,

91

governments did not fall back into excessive interventionism. It may be further hypothesised that governments with traditions of strong state planning will be less prudent with the instruments at hand.

Summarising the debate thus far, the main differences stem from the participants' belief in the benevolent working of the price mechanism. If there is a belief that under convertibility the market will create an incorrect exchange rate at which the wrong things are imported, then state intervention and a Payments Union, rather than convertibility, seem the appropriate clearing mechanisms since they facilitate control of transactions. Faith in this system is enhanced by the belief that a benevolent government can exist which knows what are the essential things which should be bought abroad, and that this government has only the well-being of its people in mind when it goes shopping abroad. The proponents of a Payments Union speak of 'structural balance of payments deficits' and 'essential imports' as opposed to 'cadillacs in Moscow' and 'exchange rates at impoverishing levels'. Conversely, opponents of the Payments Union idea prefer the market to the government.

EUROPE THEN AND RUSSIA NOW

A West European visitor's first impression after setting foot on former Soviet soil is that he or she is in a place that has been ravaged by a recent major calamity, such as a war. Perhaps that is the reason why West European postwar solutions are suggested to solve East European post-Communist problems. The differences between the two cases are manifold, however.

First, let us address the relevant differences between capitalism interrupted by a five-year war and more than seventy years of Communism. Under Communism, finance is much less relevant than in a market economy. Firms were not assessed on their profits, but on their material output. Hence they did not care whether their clients paid or not. Logically, under such a system very few resources will be devoted to finance. The main problem with payments in the former Soviet Union today is that the payments system is very much underdeveloped, and this problem has little to do with interstate relations; it exists *within* all of the Newly Independent States as much as *among* them. Surprisingly, this fact is used both as an argument in favour of a Payments Union and against it. Rosati (1993: 350) holds that 'until the domestic difficulties are overcome, an external mechanism would make no difference'. This view is unconvincing, for if the banking system is unable to set up a smooth payments and clearing regime internally, it will be *a fortiori* so externally. A state-supported centralised clearing house therefore has a point:

> Although payments will eventually be cleared and settled directly between commercial banks in the different countries as in most parts of the world, this is apparently not happening today on a scale that is large enough to fully enable trade. The reason for this failure is that in most CIS countries, the commercial banking sector is still in an embryonic state of development and lacks the technical capacities and the know-how to provide smooth interstate payments to its clients . . . there is thus a role for the Interstate Bank's multilateral payments mechanism.
>
> (AGIR 1994a: 3).

Another important difference related to history is that in the East today, prices are far more distorted, and competition has been absent for a much longer time period. 'In the FSU, convertibility with independent currencies will not only help to make payments possible, but will also introduce international prices and competition into the economy' (Fischer 1993b: 350). The situation in the former Soviet Union in 1994 is also more troubled than that of Western Europe in 1950 because stabilisation has not yet taken place. As we have argued before, this has consequences for the Payments Union, because a credit facility will be very difficult to implement under hyperinflation (Wagener and van Selm 1993: 421).

Next, the size of the area under consideration relative to the size of the world is very different. As stated, Western Europe then had enough market power to be able to improve its terms of trade if the rest of the world went along and did not retaliate. The EPU covered an area that accounted for about 70 per cent of world trade. But the East today does not have a significant share of the world market, except for trade in a few selected products, such as oil and gas.

Related to this, the propects for trade within the region are smaller for the former Soviet Union today than they were for Western Europe half a century ago. In Europe then,

> the countries were natural trading partners for reasons of proximity and history. To say that Germany was a traditional

exporter of capital goods and other European countries of consumer goods is to generalize excessively but to convey the essential point.

(Eichengreen 1993a: 329).

According to Eichengreen (1993a: 312),

> EPU was an institutional exit barrier that lent credibility to the commitment to trade and integration. Restructuring Europe along export-oriented lines was costly. Before undertaking it, policy makers wanted to be sure that Europe's commitment to free trade was permanent.

In the East today, however, the starting position is not autarky, but overintegration among the republics. There is a huge gap between the level of integration that existed in the past (van Selm and Wagener 1993) and the level of integration that can be expected in the future (van Selm 1995b).

> Proponents of the Payments Union support it as a means of slowing the collapse of trade among the republics. They have no doubt that much of that trade should disappear. Thus we are looking at a stopgap institution, one that would depend on and help re-establish the planning systems that have broken down and that should remain broken down. They probably cannot be put together, but in any case they should not be put together.

(Fischer 1993b: 349).

A more practical difference between Western Europe then and the former Soviet Union now is that the will to cooperate among the governments concerned is much smaller in the latter case. In the first two years the EPU could hardly be called a system; it was crisis management (Kaplan and Schleiminger 1989: 91–153). A considerable degree of diplomatic flexibility was needed to keep the EPU alive. The next section will make clear that this flexibility does not exist in the Soviet successor states.

Perhaps the most important difference is simply experience. The UK 1947 attempt discouraged other European states from trying to introduce a convertible currency. But the successful introduction by Estonia, Latvia and Lithuania of a convertible and fairly stable currency should show the way for the other Soviet successor states. Russia itself has managed to introduce a fairly convertible currency as well, albeit a rapidly inflating one. This is, however, not caused by the impossibility of introducing a convertible currency, but by too loose monetary politics. It may sound paradoxical, but the present position of Russia within the CIS can be compared to the US position with respect to Europe after World War II. Russia has a near-to-convertible currency. It is a creditor to all other CIS states and will perhaps remain so for quite some time. The dollar was a convertible currency and consequently the USA stayed outside the EPU. The EPU was meant to liberalise trade with the USA gradually and to introduce full convertibility later. Judging from this parallel, Russia should stay outside a CIS Payments Union. Installed only for the smaller Newly Independent States, such a scheme would, however, be stillborn.

In short, any arguments that may have existed in favour of the formation of a European Payments Union in the 1950s are much weaker in the case of the former Soviet Union in the 1990s. This is a view that even some EPU enthusiasts share: 'In the EPU area regional balance was a practical goal, at least for a limited period while economic reconstruction was in progress. Elsewhere, it would almost certainly lead to uneconomic distortion of trade patterns, discouraging economic efficiency and competitiveness' (Kaplan and Schleiminger 1989: 353). Untroubled by this, however, EU-paid advisers have stepped in and advocated the creation of a CIS Payments Union, and apparently they have convinced the CIS states of the usefulness of such an institution. The following section reviews the 'progress' that has been made.

PRACTICE: WHAT'S GOING ON?

At a meeting in Bishkek on 9 October, 1992, the CIS heads of state agreed to create the Interstate Bank, as an institution that could play the role of a clearing house as was fulfilled by the Bank for International Settlements in the EPU. This decision was confirmed at a CIS meeting on 22 January, 1993. The decision to create the Interstate Bank was thus taken at a point when the rouble zone was unravelling, but still partially intact. At the end of 1992 rouble notes depicting Lenin were still legal tender in all CIS states except in Ukraine, where since November 1992 the kupon had been the only legal tender. Bank account roubles in the twelve CIS states, however, have been inconvertible since July 1992.

The Interstate Bank treaties were drawn up with the assistance of the 'Advisory Group on Interstate Economic Relations' (AGIR,

French for 'to act'). The AGIR group was lead by Daniel Gros, a longstanding proponent of an Eastern Payments Union (see e.g. Bofinger and Gros 1992), and funded by TACIS (Technical Assistance to the Commonwealth of Independent States), the EU's assistance programme to the former Soviet Union. The role of AGIR was important, if their reports are anything to go by: 'At every occasion, AGIR explained to the non-Russian republics what was expected of them, or even what the Interstate Bank was all about to begin with' (AGIR 1994b: 4). Similar remarks in AGIR's reports confirm the notion that the Interstate Bank was created not because there was an ex-Soviet demand for it, but more because there was an EU-subsidised supply of it.

After January 1993 no concrete steps were taken actually to set up the Interstate Bank. The rouble zone kept on unravelling, however. New currencies were introduced in Kirgizstan in May 1993; in Georgia, Moldova, Turkmenistan and Azerbaidzjan in July 1993; and in Kazakhstan, Uzbekistan and Armenia in November 1993. Only Tadzjikistan remained in the rouble zone; Belarus also left, but started having second thoughts later. The 1993 currency introductions provided a new stimulus both for trying to make the Bishkek Agreement reality and for devising new schemes.

At this point, AGIR saw three reasons why the Interstate Bank was not functioning, two 'subjective' factors and one 'objective' factor.

> One of the subjective factors is the lack of understanding of the payments mechanism in many other republics, coupled with deficient information flows in those countries' governing bodies. The most prominent example of this is Ukraine. The other subjective factor is the wavering and untransparent position of the Central Bank of Russia.
>
> (AGIR 1994b: 6)

AGIR's relations with the employee of the Central Bank of Russia who was elected president of the Interstate Bank, Mr Savanin, were not optimal. For example,

> AGIR discussed progress and the way ahead with Mr Savanin on 23 November 1993. This meeting with Mr Savanin did not produce any results, except for the usual complaint by Mr

Savanin that he still does not have premises for the Interstate Bank.

And, in a footnote: 'AGIR's impression of his lack of dynamism was again confirmed' (AGIR 1994b: 7).

> The objective factor may be summarised as follows. The Interstate Bank has been the victim of a learning process in the CIS with respect to monetary relations: Russia took a number of steps that broke off its monetary relations with other republics . . . . The result of this process is that the other republics will understand that the rouble is Russian property and that they cannot take the past subsidization of their economies for granted. When this learning period is over, the Interstate Bank's payments mechanism may come to the fore again as a useful technical instrument to improve payments between independent countries with separate monetary realms.
>
> (AGIR 1994b: 6)

The IMF also expressed optimism and a positive attitude with respect to the Interstate Bank.

> Pending the decentralization of payments and the move to full and sustainable convertibility by the states in the region which have introduced national currencies, the Interstate Bank – as a multilateral clearing and settlements mechanism – can usefully serve to facilitate interstate payments.
>
> (IMF 1994: 4)

Notwithstanding the problems with getting the Interstate Bank operational, AGIR went on and started circulating a (Russian version of a) note on a construction of a Payments Union in November 1993. Discussions followed in January 1994. Here AGIR's opinion differed from the IMF's. According to the Fund,

> it will be important to ensure that the role of the Interstate Bank is limited to multilateral clearing, rather than permitting it to evolve into a Payments Union by augmenting the clearing mechanism with significant quantities of settlement credit provided either by creditor-participants or the international financial community.
>
> (IMF 1994: 19)

As disadvantages of a Payments Union, the IMF mentions that it 'could easily develop into a forum for intense bargaining over the amounts and the terms of credit', 'could well lead member states to focus their energies on expanding mutual trade to the expense of the rest of the world', 'would almost inevitably involve the creation of a new bureaucracy that – given the tradition of central planning in most states of the region, and the continuing reliance on inter-governmental trade agreements and state orders in some countries – could materially slow the progress toward decentralised market relations in interstate trade' (IMF 1994: 19). 'In sum, a Payments Union may be viewed as involving more risks than advantages' (IMF 1994: 20).

The discussions on the creation of a Payments Union continued nevertheless, and in March 1994 agreement was reached on the creation of a 'Payments Union'. However, to the despair of AGIR, in the 'concept' the Payments Union is defined as convertibility! In article 3 of the 'Concept on a Payments Union', it says that

> Countries-participants in the Payments Union ensure a regime of convertibility of their national currency in a foreign currency by everyday operations (operations, linked with the movement of goods and services). Residents will be given the possibility of acquiring foreign currencies (as the free convertibility of currencies, therefore also of national currencies of countries-participants in the Payments Union) in exchange for a national currency for the realisation of everyday operations in conjunction with national legislation. Administrative regulations for the conclusion of import transactions with juridical character will not be set up.

As a reply, AGIR wrote this note (author's translation from the Russian):

> AGIR, having taken notice of the 'concept of the Payments Union' that was signed by experts from 9 CIS countries on the 17–18 of March 1994, notes that this concept goes much further than the proposed Payments Union, because it proposes direct and full convertibility, both on current and on capital accounts. If the subscribers consider this a possibility, AGIR will of course support this measure. However, the AGIR group really does not see why, if the subscribers of this concept really want full (or Russian-style, even though that is not full) convertibility, they have not yet taken steps in this direction, without a treaty. Thus,

Table 7.2 Settlements among FSU countries (%)

	1993	1994	1995
Bilateral interstate barter/clearing	50	30	15
Settlements through correspondent accounts in national central banks	20	15	5
Settlements in national currencies through commercial banks	15	35	55
Barter, clearing and other forms of counter trade	10	10	10
Settlements in hard currency	5	10	15

Source: Russian Economic Trends (1995, no.3: 35). The data for 1995 are forecasts

while hoping that the present treaty will be realised in practice, AGIR is sceptical about this really happening.

It seems that all this has been too much for AGIR and that they have surrendered. 'AGIR will now try to support the creation of a private sector system that could make interstate payments quicker and more reliable' (AGIR 1994c: 1). In a concluding report, *The Interstate Bank: Genesis and Demise*, AGIR still defends the Payments Union as a good idea. The following reasons for its failure are given: 'most CIS states were only interested in obtaining cheap credit and/or cheap oil from Russia', 'advantages of an efficient payments system were dimly perceived', 'there is a deep seated tendency in many CIS countries to wait for Russia to take the initiative', and 'it has proved extremely difficult to create any type of public institution in Russia' (Gros 1994: 3–4). Here the story ends, and it is unlikely to be continued.

Meanwhile, commercial banks have filled the gap that the Interstate Bank left open. As can be seen from Table 7.2, current account transactions among former Soviet republics are increasingly settled in national currencies through commercial banks.

CONCLUSION

This chapter has shown that the theoretical objections to and the practical problems related to the CIS Interstate Bank/Payments Union are manifold. The account of the European Payments Union may not be a success story after all, and the circumstances in the former Soviet Union today are very different from what they were in Western Europe in 1950. If any parallels can be drawn, the position of Russia is more like the European than the American position after the Second World War, which implies that it has only a passive interest in a Payments Union. In practice, a 'Payments Union' has been created on paper, but many officials in the former Soviet Union have only vague notions of what it is supposed to do and nobody is really pushing the idea, especially since EU-paid advisers pulled out of the scheme in utter frustration.

Even if properly installed and operative, a CIS Payments Union would hardly repeat the EPU success. The participating governments are not particularly known for their commitment to trade liberalisation. A CIS Payments Union would at best be a replication of CMEA in which, for understandable reasons, nobody seems to be really interested.

The most important reason why nothing is happening may be the general ex-Soviet governments' treaty implementation problem. In that sense, the 'Bishkek Agreement' and the 'Concept on a Payments Union' are no different from the Monetary Union between Russia and Belarus of 1994 and the other attempts to keep alive or revive the rouble zone. Pretty words, but in real life nobody feels bound by them. That is a development that is far more worrying than the fact that there is no Interstate Bank or Payments Union functioning today.

8

THE SOVIET UNION AS A REDISTRIBUTOR

INTRODUCTION

In this chapter we turn to a different aspect of the break-up of the Soviet Union: the end of fiscal redistribution. As we made clear in Chapter 1, redistribution of income among the parts of a single state is usually far more important than redistribution among independent states. Hence, we expect a change in the pattern of income redistribution on account of Soviet break-up. We discussed the magnitude of redistribution flows briefly in Chapter 2. Here we present a more detailed study.

An interesting result is that in the pattern of income redistribution, tendencies towards disintegration can be traced long before August 1991 or even 1985, Gorbachev's first year in power. The data suggest that the aim of reaching equality in the republics' levels of economic development was given up before 1985. In this chapter, we assess Soviet interrepublican capital transfers over the 1966–91 time interval. The methodology used for this purpose is explained in the next section. The magnitude of the capital transfers turns out to be surprisingly high, when taken both as a percentage of national product and in an international context.

On the pattern of capital redistribution, we argue in the third section that these transfers flowed from 'rich' to 'poor' up to 1978, whereas later on this pattern failed to hold well. This is attributed to a shift in central government policy priorities from equality to output maximisation. In all likelihood, this shift should be interpreted as an attempt to improve the faltering overall Soviet growth performance. The effects of this policy change on the inequality in economic development among the republics is described in the fourth section. Inequality was relatively stable up to 1983 and

101

increased rapidly from that year onwards. Hence, we can conclude that economic Soviet disintegration preceded political Soviet disintegration and took off prior to the advent of perestroika. Economic disintegration might very well have stimulated and accelerated political disintegration.

Future prospects for interrepublican capital transfers and the resulting inequality levels are discussed in the penultimate section. Now that the Soviet Union has vanished, interrepublican capital transfers are expected to come to a complete halt soon. Because of this, the level of interrepublican inequality can be expected to increase further. The main findings of the analysis are summarised in the concluding section.

CAPITAL TRANSFERS: METHODOLOGY AND RESULTS

In the economic literature some confusion exists with respect to the term 'capital transfer'. Here we define a capital transfer as any imbalance in goods exchange that is not covered by a shipment of reserves (gold and foreign exchange). This implies that capital transfers are accompanied either by a coverage with bonds or by no coverage with financial assets at all. The latter case, which is particularly relevant here, is called an unrequited transfer.

The Soviet Union was a planned economy. Interrepublican capital flows were not caused by interest or risk differentials, but were the result of imbalances in the exchange of goods among the republics as planned by the central government. Such imbalances did not lead to liabilities on the receiver's side or assets on the donor's side. A Soviet republic could 'use' more than 'produce' without accumulating debts. Therefore imbalances in interrepublican goods exchange can be interpreted as unrequited capital transfers.

As we explained in Chapter 4, different methods of estimating Soviet interrepublican capital transfers can be employed. If statistics on goods exchange are available they should be used to assess republican 'trade balances' (and hence capital transfers) directly. Unfortunately, the republican input–output tables necessary to obtain data on interrepublican goods exchange were compiled only once every five years. National income accounting statistics can be used to obtain a time series. In Table 4.3, we presented the republics' goods exchange balances and national income balances for 1988 to show that the latter is quite a good proxy for the former. The coefficient of correlation between the two series turned out to be 97 per cent. In Table 4.4 we presented a 1966–91 capital transfers time series.

The first conclusion to be drawn from these data is that the magnitude of Soviet interrepublican capital transfers is quite large. Several republics receive or donate more than 10 per cent of their NIP over prolonged periods of time. The magnitude of Soviet interrepublican capital transfers can be put into a context by comparing the USSR data to some EU statistics. Unrequited capital transfers from EU member states seldom exceed 1 per cent of their GNP. It could be argued that as we used imbalances in goods exchange among Soviet republics to assess their capital transfers, we should use the same method in the case of the EU. EU member states' goods imbalances as a percentage of GNP are usually in the range of 0 to 4 per cent. These figures do not come close to the Soviet republics' percentages.[1]

Next, we turn to the pattern of Soviet interrepublican capital transfers. Over the whole range of our time series, the Slavic republics and Azerbaidzjan are donors, whereas the Central Asian republics except Turkmenistan are receivers. The Baltic republics all developed from donors to receivers in about 1980. For the remaining republics, the picture is less clear. Among the donor republics, Azerbaidzjan stands out with transfers to NIP of more than 20 per cent annually. Kazakhstan is the most heavily subsidised republic, receiving transfers up to 30 per cent of its NIP. Capital transfers this large definitely have a significant impact on overall economic performance.

A SHIFT IN INVESTMENT PRIORITIES

The pattern of interrepublican capital redistribution reflects Soviet investment decisions. These decisions were first of all ruled by sectoral considerations, and second only by regional considerations.[2] Moreover, Soviet capital allocation was not determined by a single planner or planning board, but rather the result of the decisions made by a number of seemingly independently operating ministries.[3] Nevertheless, the spatial aspect of the Soviet economy was important enough and the degree of centralisation of Soviet power was high enough to justify a closer look at the officially proclaimed locational principles of Soviet investment policy. Most

Soviet regional investment rules were derived directly from the works of Engels and Lenin. These 'principles of location of productive forces' are:

1 Location of enterprises either near the raw material sources or near the centres of consumption according to minimal cost of production and transport.
2 Even distribution of economic activity throughout the country.
3 Rational division of labour between economic regions, and complex development of the economy of each region.
4 Raising of the economic and cultural level of all backward national areas to that of the most advanced.
5 Elimination of the distinction between town and country.
6 Strengthening of the defence potential of the country.
7 The international division of labour within the socialist bloc (Dyker 1983: 114).

These principles can be subdivided into three categories: the first is oriented towards output maximisation, the second, fourth and fifth are equality oriented, and the last two may be described as geo-political, whereas the status of principle 3 is somewhat unclear.[4] Principle 6 became less important in regional investment planning after 1945 owing to warfare developments.[5] Moreover, it is unclear why and how the promotion of the international division of labour within the socialist bloc (principle 7) influences intra-USSR capital redistribution. This leaves us with 'output maximisation' and 'equality' as policy objectives. In the appendix to this chapter, a simple example is provided to show that these aims are likely to have been rivals in the Soviet context. Deciding which of these two was more important in actual Soviet decision making is an empirical matter.

In Table 8.1, we present data on the relation between wealth and transfers. We split up the fifteen republics according to their wealth (measured in NIP per capita) in 1980. The Baltic republics, Russia and Belarus are the relatively rich, the Central Asian republics (excluding Kazakhstan) are the relatively poor, whereas the remaining republics make up the average wealth group.

A glance at the data suggests that the 1966–78 transfers fit quite well a redistribution of Soviet national income from the more developed republics to the lesser developed republics. Furthermore, it seems that this is not true for the later time intervals. We calculated Spearman rank correlation coefficients for the three

Table 8.1 The republics' wealth related to capital transfers, 1966–91

	1966–78		1979–86		1987–91	
	NIP/cap.	K/NIP	NIP/cap.	K/NIP	NIP/cap.	K/NIP
Latvia	133.0	5.5	129.1	4.6	125.8	−2.2
Estonia	130.2	0.1	121.8	−5.3	127.5	−11.5
Russia	111.4	5.6	112.7	1.4	119.3	3.3
Belarus	99.3	10.4	112.0	16.5	118.3	9.8
Lithuania	110.8	22.2	102.0	−3.4	107.4	−7.4
Armenia	81.6	0.2	93.3	12.4	83.9	−1.3
Georgia	74.7	−5.2	95.1	6.1	80.6	0.6
Ukraine	96.1	6.5	89.9	5.5	90.1	1.7
Moldova	82.9	6.5	86.6	4.8	84.4	−4.1
Azerbaidzjan	66.0	7.9	82.5	22.4	68.0	15.4
Kazakhstan	82.0	−18.9	76.5	−20.2	76.6	−20.3
Turkmenistan	75.8	2.6	68.2	1.0	59.7	−4.3
Uzbekistan	62.5	−6.2	60.7	−5.4	47.3	−15.7
Kirgizstan	65.2	−12.9	59.8	−8.6	54.1	−21.6
Tadzjikistan	59.0	−9.9	52.3	−9.4	43.1	−12.5

Sources: National income produed per capita (NIP/cap.) from various Goskomstat sources, USSR = 100; capital transfers as a percentage of NIP (K/NIP) derived from Table 4.4

time intervals 1966–78, 1979–86 and 1987–91 to corroborate our feelings that the 'rich-to-poor' thesis received relatively strong support during the first time interval, and relatively weak support afterwards. The Spearman ρ are 0.500, 0.432 and 0.432 for the 1966–78, 1979–86 and 1987–91 time intervals respectively. Only the first coefficient stands a t-test at the common 95 per cent probability level. Yet, it must be noted that the statistical evidence is rather weak as the Spearman ρ and the t-values are rather similar for all periods.[6] Still, the 'rich-to-poor' thesis holds better for the 1966–78 period than afterwards.

We conclude that there is some empirical evidence that 'output maximisation' gradually overtook 'equality' as the leading principle of Soviet regional investment policy. This conclusion is in line with other evidence available. For example, Breznjev is reported to have claimed that 'the problem of equalizing the levels of development of the national republics has in the main been solved' (Holubnychy 1973: 25). Probst, the late doyen of Soviet regional policy, dismisses the principle of equalising these levels in his later work (Dyker 1983: 117). Finally, in an ordinary least squares (OLS) regression analysis for investment in the Soviet republics for 1980–88, Burkett used 'efficiency','equality' and 'defense' as variables and found that only 'efficiency' was significant (Burkett 1992: 162).

What reason could there have been for the Soviet leadership to put more emphasis on output maximisation and less on promoting interrepublican equality from the late 1970s onwards? The central planners' dissatisfaction with overall Soviet growth performance is likely to have played an important role here. According to a recent Soviet estimate, GNP growth declined from 4.2 per cent per year over the period 1960–70 to 3.2 per cent for 1970–5, 1.0 per cent for 1975–80 and 0.6 per cent for 1980–5.[7] We hypothesise that in order to reverse this trend, the central authorities stopped distributing capital from rich to poor and started to invest in promising economic sectors, especially energy. Narzikulov (1992: 8) reports that in the early 1970s, the Central Asian region received 2.5 times more investment resources than did the Tyumen (the oil region) and Tomsk oblasts; by the mid 1980s the volume of these two investment flows became about equal.[8] This supports our thesis that Soviet capital was redirected from the poor to the promising in an attempt to improve overall Soviet economic performance. Whether this was successful or a waste of resources is still an open question.

The differences between the pattern of transfers in the 1979–86 period versus the 1987–91 period should be interpreted as a change in Soviet overall economic policy rather than a change in investment policy. After a long period of stability in relative Soviet prices, the Soviet leaders attempted to open up the economy and to bring Soviet relative prices more in line with world market relative prices in the later years of perestroika. The price of raw materials to consumer goods was raised, and hence the balance of national income of the exporter of raw materials *pur sang*, the Russian Federation, improved substantially to the disadvantage of most of the other republics' accounts.[9]

THE EFFECTS OF CAPITAL TRANSFERS: DISPERSION TRENDS IN THE SOVIET REPUBLICS' LEVELS OF DEVELOPMENT

Estimates of the dispersion of levels of development of the Soviet republics have been made for various years during the existence of the Soviet Union and even before its birth.[10] We present estimates of dispersion for our 1966–91 time period. The variable that we use is national income per capita, as this is the most comprehensive and most widely used indicator of the level of development.[11] In order to assess dispersion trends, we use two measures: Williamson's coefficient of variation and Theil's more recent entropy measure of inequality (Theil 1967).

The coefficient of variation was calculated according to the following formula:

$$V_w = \frac{\sqrt{\Sigma(y_i - \bar{y})^2 \, (f_i/n)}}{\bar{y}} \tag{8.1}$$

where f_i denotes the population of the ith republic, n denotes national population, y_i denotes per capita NIP of the ith republic, and $\bar{y}$ per capita NIP for the whole country. Calculating inequality using the entropy measure is slightly more complicated. First, it is necessary to calculate for all republics a variable p_i, that is defined as

$$p_i = \frac{y_i}{\Sigma y_i} \tag{8.2}$$

with y_i denoting a republic's NIP per capita and Σy_i denoting the sum of the republics' NIP per capita. Entropy is given by the following equation as derived by Theil:

$$E(y) = \Sigma \, p_i \log_2(1/p_i) \tag{8.3}$$

The maximum value of this equation is $\log_2 15$, 15 being the number of Soviet republics, when the proportions are the same for all republics, and with a minimum value of zero. An inequality measure can be obtained from equation (8.3) by subtracting $E(y)$ from $\log_2 15$ as this number represents perfect equality between the republics. Hence, inequality can be defined as

$$I(y) = \log_2 15 - \Sigma \, p_i \log_2(1/p_i) \tag{8.4}$$

When applied to calculating the dispersion in the levels of development of the Soviet republics, these two measures render similar results. We found that up to 1983, the degree of inequality is quite stable. From 1983 onwards, however, the degree of inequality rises quickly and steeply.[12]

The increased dispersion found is not accompanied by significant changes in the order of the republics according to their wealth measured in national income produced per capita, as can be seen from Table 8.1. In order to be sure, we calculated Spearman rank correlation coefficients for the order of the republics according to their wealth in 1970, 1980 and 1990. For 1970–80, 1980–90 and 1970–90 these were, respectively, 0.857, 0.961 and 0.939. All these coefficients show a very high significance, i.e. a significance at the highest probability levels reported, implying that the increased inequality that we found in both measures of inequality is definitely not accompanied by a change in the relative positions of the republics. In the 1980s, the rich became richer and the poor became poorer.

Linking the Soviet trends in inequality to the changing pattern of transfers is quite straightforward. As we have seen, transfers went from rich to poor in the 1960s and 1970s; in the 1980s and 1990s, this pattern changed. The logical conclusion seems to be that in the 1960s and the 1970s, Soviet investment policy, directed at equality, succeeded in combating nascent tendencies towards increasing inequality. When the direction of the transfers changed, owing to a shift in policy, a process of increasing interrepublican inequality started only a couple of years later. This trend of increasing inequality continued in the last years of the Union's existence.

TRANSFERS AFTER THE BREAK-UP OF THE SOVIET UNION

The break-up of the Soviet Union has had significant implications for both the mechanism and the pattern of interrepublican capital redistribution. A central planner that governs interrepublican goods exchange and thereby redistributes capital no longer exists. Also, there is no longer a common budget that can be used to redistribute income. Nevertheless, via a number of channels transfers continued to be made.

From 1992 onwards, many bilateral trade agreements between Soviet successor states were agreed upon. In principle these agreements balanced trade flows bilaterally. In practice, however,

> all the other CIS countries delivered far less to Russia than they
> had promised, while Russia came closer to meeting its delivery

targets. In 1992, Russia had a trade surplus with every CIS
state, and in 1993 with all but Azerbaidzjan and Uzbekistan.
(Åslund 1995: 121)

The overall trade surplus of Russia *vis-à-vis* the other successor
states was 5.3 per cent of Russian GNP in 1992 and 3.2 per cent in
1993 (Åslund 1995: 123). Such surpluses led to Russian financial
claims on the other republics; however, the value of these claims is
dubious (see below).

In fact, the transfers that Russia handed out to the other successor states via trade flows were higher still, because of the fact
that the prices that were charged for energy remained lower than
world market prices. 'In 1992 the intra-CIS price for crude oil was
only 10.3 per cent of the price Russia obtained on world markets,
while that of natural gas was only 8.1 per cent of the extra-CIS
export price' (Smith 1995: 245). Gradually, energy prices in intra-
CIS trade were brought more in line with world market prices, but
in mid 1994 the price for gas in intra-CIS trade was still only 77 per
cent of the world market price (Smith 1995: 245).

Apart from these 'real', i.e. trade-related transfers, financial
transfers also continued to exist. For example, the Central Bank
of Russia simply continued to ship large volumes of cash to other
former Soviet republics in 1993. Especially Kazakhstan and Turkmenistan received lots of roubles in the first half of 1993 (Åslund
1995: 129). The IMF (1994: 26) estimates that the shipments of
roubles from Russia to other successor states amounted to 3.2 per
cent of Russian GDP in 1992.

In addition, the Russian Central Bank continued to give credits
to other Soviet successor states' central banks in 1992 and 1993
(IMF 1994: 11). These credit flows are reported to have amounted
to 8.5 per cent of Russian GNP in 1992 and 1.1 per cent in 1993
(IMF 1994: 25). Until July 1992, the Central Bank of Russia did not
put limits on its credits to other successor states, although it did
monitor them from January 1992. After July 1992, credits were no
longer granted automatically and *ex post*, but had to be negotiated
ex ante with the Central Bank of Russia and were called 'technical
credits' (IMF 1994: 34). New technical credits were agreed on at
the beginning of 1993, and ran out in May 1993. Since then the
practice has been virtually stopped.

Of these four flows, only the price channel has led to immediate
and irretrievable Russian subsidies to other republics. The other

forms of transfers have been consolidated into debts. On 30 June 1993, the debt was agreed to be $5.1 billion (CER 1995a: 36). In October 1995, the Ministry for Co-operation between CIS countries put the figure at $9 billion. Of this amount, $5.8 billion were 'state credits' (including the 'technical credits') and $3.2 billion were trade credits (CER 1995b: 36). The repayment of these debts has thus far been problematic: 'for example, in 1994 only $12 million out of a total of $865 million was actually repaid' (CER 1995a: 36). By far the largest debtor is Ukraine (CER 1995a: 36; 1995b: 36). If these debts turn out to be worthless, then the other three channels mentioned above should also be regarded as sources of Russian transfers to other successor states.

Although the analysis of post-Soviet transfers among the successor states is highly complex, a few broad conclusions can be drawn. First, channels for subsidies continued to exist even without a common budget and a central planner that decides on goods flows. Second, the subsidies were probably still huge in 1992, but have been reduced since then. The remaining transfers are a temporary phenomenon; they can be expected to come to a complete halt.

The ending of interrepublican capital transfers will require significant adjustment from the majority of the former Soviet republics. The deficit republics must either increase their exports or reduce their imports. In the short run, reducing imports is easier than increasing exports. Hence, many republics will have to cut their imports significantly. An indication of the magnitude of the adjustments required can be obtained by recalculating 1988 interrepublican goods exchange using world market prices. We cannot simply use the trade balances of Table 4.3 here, because in this table, interrepublican trade is measured in internal Soviet prices and extra-USSR trade is measured in world market prices. However, current interrepublican trade also uses world market prices. Hence, interrepublican trade balances should be recalculated. Such an exercise was performed in Table 4.6.

These data should not be interpreted as a prediction of future trade imbalances. Obviously, changing the price structure would also change the structure of goods exchange among republics. However, if calculated correctly, they do give an indication of the huge changes in the 1988 pattern of goods exchange that are necessary to achieve a minimum amount of equilibrium on the republics' trade balances, because the trade deficits are extremely high for many republics. The data indicate that Lithuania, Moldova and Estonia will reach the traditional danger threshold of 40 per cent external debt to GNP within two years if goods flows remain unaltered.[13]

Especially the Central Asian republics will have to face a period of severe economic restructuring. Western aid programmes typically amount to some 5 per cent of the recipient's GNP and never approach 20 per cent, which is about the size of the transfers that the Soviet Union made to Kirgizstan or Uzbekistan. The position of the Baltic republics seems to be somewhat more favourable. Their prospects for attracting private foreign capital as a substitute for Soviet transfers are much better, because of their higher political stability and level of economic development and industrialisation. This leads us to the conclusion that the impact of the ending of interrepublican capital transfers on interrepublican equality in levels of development can be expected to be significant. Both the transfers to the 'poor' Central Asian republics and the transfers to the 'rich' Baltic republics will come to a halt, but it will prove to be more difficult to find compensation for the former than for the latter. Hence, we expect a further increase in inequality in economic development among the republics in the 1990s.

CONCLUSION

We suggest the following interpretation of the results obtained. In the 1960s and 1970s, Soviet investment policy, directed at equality, succeeded in combating nascent tendencies towards increasing inequality. Gradually, however, 'output maximisation' gained in importance relative to 'equality'. In the late 1970s, Soviet planners started to perceive their economic growth rates as insufficient. Capital redistribution from rich to poor was done away with so as to improve the overall Soviet economic performance, and a process of increasing interrepublican economic inequality started only a couple of years later. After 1985, the effort to accelerate Soviet economic growth ('output maximisation' in a dynamic setting) came to be referred to by the term *uskoreniye*. By increasing interrepublican economic inequality, this policy released latent centrifugal forces. We may cautiously conclude that the dissolution of the Soviet empire should be attributed not only to perestroika, but also to *uskoreniye*. In the future, capital transfers can be expected to come to a complete halt. As a result, interrepublican inequality will further increase.

APPENDIX: OUTPUT MAXIMISATION VERSUS EQUALITY

Here we provide a simple example to show that under a few plausible assumptions, the objectives of output maximisation and equality were rivals in the Soviet context. It is shown that if the central planner allocates capital so as to maximise the combined output of regions (1) and (2), this results in unequal levels of production per capita. Maximising total output implies that capital is allocated so that its marginal productivity is equal in the two regions. By doing so, both the marginal and the average productivity of labour differ among the regions.

Assume a more developed region (1) and a less developed region (2). In their Cobb–Douglas production functions, this difference in economic development is expressed in their coefficient for technology ($\delta > 1$). K denotes total capital available. We assume that capital can move freely from one region to the other, whereas labour is immobile. This assumption is not unrealistic in the Soviet setting: control over the economy was fully centralised in Moscow, whereas the post-Stalin planner's power to reallocate labour was limited. K_1 is allocated in region (1), the rest, $K - K_1$, in region (2). Furthermore, we assume for reasons of simplicity the amount of labour available, L, and total population, P, in both regions to be equal: $L_2 = L_1$ and $P_2 = P_1$. Also, we assume the labour share of the population to be equal, $L = \sigma P$, for both regions with $0 < \sigma < 1$, and $a = \frac{1}{2}$. Then, we have

$$Y_1 = \delta b K_1^{\frac{1}{2}} L_1^{\frac{1}{2}} \tag{A8.1}$$

$$Y_2 = b(K - K_1)^{\frac{1}{2}} L_1^{\frac{1}{2}} \tag{A8.2}$$

with b, K and $L > 0$. Total national product is

$$Y = Y_1 + Y_2 = \delta b K_1^{\frac{1}{2}} L_1^{\frac{1}{2}} + b(K - K_1)^{\frac{1}{2}} L_1^{\frac{1}{2}}$$

Maximising this output implies that

$$dY/dK_1 = \tfrac{1}{2}\delta b K_1^{-\frac{1}{2}} L_1^{\frac{1}{2}} - \tfrac{1}{2}b(K - K_1)^{-\frac{1}{2}} L_1^{\frac{1}{2}} = 0$$

which gives

$$\delta K_1^{-\frac{1}{2}} = (K - K_1)^{-\frac{1}{2}}$$

or

$$(1/\delta^2)K = K - K_1$$

Substituting this expression in equation (A8.2) gives us

$$Y_1 = \delta b K_1^{1/2} L_1^{1/2} \qquad (A8.1')$$

$$Y_2 = b(1/\delta^2)^{1/2} K_1^{1/2} L_1^{1/2} \qquad (A8.2')$$

which leads to $Y_1 = \delta^2 Y_2$. With $\delta > 1$, $L_1 = L_2$ and $L = \sigma P$ it follows that $(Y/P)_1 > (Y/P)_2$.

Hence, the objectives of maximising output and obtaining regional equality are, considering the high levels of inequality in Soviet regional development, likely to have been conflicting at least to some extent.

9

THE NEWLY INDEPENDENT
STATES IN TRANSITION

INTRODUCTION

As a final element in the study of the economics of Soviet break-up, we now turn to the different transition strategies developed in the Newly Independent States. As we have seen in Chapter 1, states matter because states choose their preferred economic system, or more precisely in the present context, states matter because they choose the speed and the method of the *transition* to their preferred economic system. Before break-up, all republics had to follow the reform plans as they were dictated from Moscow in the name of perestroika. The new situation enables the republics to do better or worse than Moscow in transforming their economies and creating market economies. We briefly discussed a few elements of transition in Chapter 2. Here we study the issue somewhat more extensively.

We concentrate on the three central elements of transition, i.e. stabilisation, liberalisation and privatisation, in the next three sections respectively. We briefly discuss the importance of price stability, price and trade liberalisation and private ownership in theory as well as the relevant Soviet inheritance. Subsequently the developments in the Newly Independent States since 1992 are dealt with. It is found that progress in some Newly Independent States has been considerably more substantial than in others.

STABILISATION

What are the elements of a transition from a planned economy to a market economy? A comparative study of the essentials of the planned economy on the one hand, and the market economy on the other, should lead to an answer. Major differences between the

114

two systems are, for example, that under Communism prices are set by the government, whereas under capitalism they are determined by market forces. Also, under Communism all enterprises are state property, whereas in a market economy most enterprises are privately owned. This immediately points to the need to liberate prices and to privatise state enterprises as elements of a comprehensive transition programme.

Price-level stabilisation is different from liberalisation and privatisation in the sense that it is not necessarily part of a transition programme. The need for stabilisation as it arises in a transition programme is not caused by intrinsic differences between capitalism and Communism, but rather by the specific way in which Communism collapsed. Obviously, prices are stable as long as they are fixed by the government; in that sense a stabilisation problem is related to the transition from Communism to capitalism. But if the Communist planners had kept the amount of money in circulation in balance with the amount of goods available, then the freeing of prices would lead only to a change in relative prices, and not to a general jump in the price level. In some countries this is what happened: for example, the liberalisation of prices in Czechoslovakia was followed by only a minor increase in the price level. Prices were liberalised in January 1991, and the inflation rate over all of 1991 was only 57.7 per cent (Gros and Steinherr 1995: 155). In 1992, it was down to 10.8 per cent. The Czechoslovak case proves that high inflation, and hence the need for a stabilisation programme, is not an intrinsic aspect of a transition from Communism to capitalism.

However, other Communist states built up a huge 'monetary overhang' during the last years of their existence. Weakened governments were no longer able to restrain wage demands; with prices and the amount of goods produced constant, this led to suppressed inflation. The Soviet Union is in this group of countries. Macro-economic balances, carefully guarded by generations of Soviet planners, were lost under Gorbachev (Gaidar 1995: 5). In 1991, the economy was overshadowed by a significant monetary overhang. Various attempts were made to deal with the problem. In January 1991, all 50 and 100 rouble bills were taken out of circulation so as to reduce the money supply, but the attempt failed miserably, and only a few per cent of the total money supply was captured. In April of that year, prices were increased by an average of 60 per cent. This relieved the problem somewhat, but did not

115

solve it. The measures taken to reduce the monetary overhang made the government highly unpopular. No further attempts were made to solve the problem; as a result, fewer and fewer goods were available in the shops at the official prices.

Gaidar's decision to free prices in January 1992 therefore brought about a huge jump in the price level. In that month alone, prices rose by 245 per cent in Russia. With the porous borders that existed between the Newly Independent States (at that time really 'newly independent', since the Soviet Union had been dissolved only a week before), the other republics had no choice but to free the prices of their tradable goods as well. In 1992, all ex-USSR republics faced inflation percentages in the hundreds or thousands. The initial jump removed the monetary overhang, but was not the end of the inflation problem in the former Soviet Union. As can be seen from Table 9.1, in no less than half of the republics 1993 inflation was even worse than that of 1992. Most republics were still using the rouble for most of that year; only the ones that had left the rouble zone had an opportunity to protect the value of their currency. This opportunity was used by the three Baltic republics and abused by Ukraine, one of the inflation champions of 1993.

Continued inflation after an initial price shock is caused by poor

Table 9.1 Consumer price inflation

	1991	1992	1993	1994	1995*
Russia	144	2,318	841	203	145
Ukraine	161	2,000	10,155	401	150
Belarus	93	1,558	1,994	1,875	260
Uzbekistan	169	910	885	423	155
Kazakhstan	150	2,567	2,169	1,160	60
Georgia	131	1,463	7,492	7,380	25
Azerbaidzjan	126	1,395	1,294	1,788	100
Lithuania	345	1,175	189	45	30
Moldova	162	2,198	837	98	20
Latvia	262	958	35	26	23
Kirgizstan	170	1,771	1,366	87	25
Tadzjikistan	204	1,364	7,344	5	240
Armenia	25	1,341	10,996	1,885	45
Turkmenistan	155	644	9,750	1,100	2,500
Estonia	304	954	36	42	22

Source: EBRD (1995: 186)   * = projection

government policy. A necessary condition for price stabilisation is prudency as regards economic 'fundamentals'. Money creation should be limited, as should the government's budget deficit. These two variables are closely related in an economy with a poorly developed capital market, because deficits that cannot be financed with bonds will have to be financed either with foreign aid or with the printing press. The central bank, as the issuer of money and credit, plays a vital role. If the director of the central bank is uninterested in keeping inflation under control and extends credit to anyone who claims that they can use it to increase production, stabilisation does not stand a chance. This was to some extent the case in Russia until October 1994 with Viktor Gerashchenko as chairman of the central bank. Ukraine is another example. 'For most of the 1990–94 period, the government was demonstrably uninterested in macro-economic stabilisation', but in 1995, 'good progress was made thanks to the steadfastness of the Central Banker, Victor Yushchenko' (Tedstrom 1995: 52). Tedstrom (1995: 55) concludes that macro-economic stabilisation is easy to achieve: 'only two people have to agree on tight monetary policy, the President and the Central Banker'.

The importance of getting the fundamentals right is made especially clear in an article by Illarionov (1996). He found strong correlations between inflation rates, money creation (in M2) and budget deficits for the fifteen Soviet successor states. The correlation between M2 and inflation is so strong that any other factors are practically ruled out as causes of inflation (Illarionov 1996: 70). The overall correlation between budget deficit on the one hand and money emission and inflation on the other is also fairly strong, with a few exceptions caused by non-monetary financing of budget deficits, especially via foreign credits (Illarionov 1996: 71).

A difficulty in interpreting the inflation rates in Table 9.1 is presented by the fact that not all republics liberalised prices to the same extent at the same time (see Table 9.2). For example, the fact that Baltic inflation in 1991 was higher than inflation in the other republics was caused by a partial liberalisation of prices in the three Baltic republics (Illarionov 1996: 68). However, by 1995 all republics had freed their prices to more or less the same extent, with the sole exception of Turkmenistan (see Table 9.2). Differences in inflation rates in 1995 are hence fully attributable to differences in macro-economic policies.

The main reason that inflation is gradually coming down is a tightening of fiscal policy after huge deficits in the first years of transition. The ratio of fiscal revenues to GDP typically dropped by ten percentage points in the early reform years from a pre-transition level of, on average, 40 per cent because traditional sources of income decreased (EBRD 1996: 7). For example, taxes on profit declined because of the transitional recession that all ex-Communist states experienced. At the same time, new expenditures such as unemployment benefits were introduced. Massive expenditure cuts, especially through a reduction in consumer and enterprise subsidies, took place in most of the CIS countries only in 1994–5. For example, the ratio of government expenditure to GNP between 1993 and 1995 declined from 69 per cent to 26 per cent in Armenia, from 58 per cent to 30 per cent in Azerbaidzjan, and from 46 per cent to 13 per cent in Georgia (EBRD 1996: 7). By reducing expenses, these governments reduced their budget deficits to single-digit levels in 1995 (Illarionov 1996: 71). Russia and Ukraine also further reduced their government budget deficits in 1995, but this was to some extent achieved via the accumulation of government arrears on payments obligations and may therefore pose a problem for future government budgets and hence future inflation (EBRD 1996: 7).

Why is it important to control inflation? In the post-Soviet context, raising this question is by no means superfluous. Opinions such as 'certainly, inflation is a serious problem, but Russians know how to work and live with it' (Mau 1992: 269) are frequently expressed. Reformers have formulated replies. For example, 'extreme inflation tends to be unstable and thus unpredictable, and relative prices shift fast in an equally arbitrary fashion. Therefore, high inflation typically leads to low investment and thus declining GNP' (Åslund 1994: 25). Moreover, 'inflation is the most regressive of taxes' (Åslund 1994: 26). Stabilisation is also important for micro-economic reasons. 'Enterprise managers will only rarely attempt to restructure their enterprises before they are convinced that money has become scarce and that the government will not bail them out' (Åslund 1995: 176). In short, there are reasons enough to try to control inflation, in Russia as well as anywhere else in the ex-USSR.

We can conclude that in the first years of transition the stabilisation policies of some republics were much more successful than those of others. Whereas some republics had already managed to bring their inflation rates under control by 1993 (Estonia and

Latvia), other were still struggling in 1995 (especially Turkmenistan). This spread in inflation rates is an important economic effect of the break-up of the Soviet Union into fifteen independent states. In a single country with a single currency, only marginal differences in the rate of inflation among parts of the country are possible.

LIBERALISATION

The need for a liberalisation policy follows immediately from a comparison between a planned and a market economy. For the internal economy, liberalisation means that prices must be freed, and the right to set up or end an enterprise or to conclude a contract should be granted. Externally, liberalisation implies that all economic agents have the right to exchange domestic currency for foreign currency and also have the right to use foreign currency for purchases abroad. The foreign trade monopoly that all East European Communist governments had must be abolished, and current account convertibility should be established.

Why are free prices important? In micro-economic terms, flexible prices are needed to bring forth an equilibrium in which the marginal costs of producers equal the marginal benefits of consumers. The Polish economist Oskar Lange (1936) has argued that a superplanner could obtain the same result, if only all marginal cost and utility schedules were known to the planner. This may be a valid point in theory, but in practice it is impossible, not least because in a dynamic economy technology and tastes, and hence costs and utilities, are subject to constant change. Changing prices in a planned economy turned out to be very difficult, though. In the Soviet Union, this was done only rarely.

> A general review of prices is undertaken at long intervals (e.g. 1955, 1967, 1981) which means that, even if they do bear some relation to cost in the first year of operation, they soon cease to have such a relation as costs alter . . . . In other words, the proposition that one can flexibly control millions of prices is clearly incorrect.
>
> (Nove 1991: 109)

Therefore, controlled prices cannot balance costs and benefits and hence lead to resource misallocation.

In the Soviet Union, resource misallocation manifested itself especially in the production and consumption of far too much steel and energy, and far too little services like retailing and banking. Lipton and Sachs (1992: 219) found that steel output per unit of GNP was fifteen times higher in the USSR than in the USA in 1988, and that energy consumption per unit of GNP was almost six times higher in the USSR. On the flip side, only 13.9 per cent of the work force was employed in services, and the number of shops per 10,000 people was only a third of that in the USA (Lipton and Sachs 1992: 219). Liberalisation of the USSR economy should therefore lead one to expect the production and consumption of less steel and energy and more services, and it did.

The potential benefits of price liberalisation in the case of the Soviet Union were high. Gros and Steinherr (1995: 118) have made a rough estimate of the welfare gains to be obtained by liberalising energy prices in the former Soviet Union, and put the figure at a minimum of $60 billion per year. The problem with price liberalisation is that prices are often used not for maximising efficiency, but for redistributing income. This is especially true for the former USSR. In order to increase equality, prices of housing (rents), food and energy were held down, whereas 'luxury goods' were priced high. An economist's verdict on such policies is that the aim may be noble but the method is wrong. By keeping prices artificially low, both the incentive to produce the goods and the incentive to consume them in a non-wasteful way are too small. Redistributing income via a lump sum (income) transfer should generally be preferred over redistribution via prices.

Price liberalisation in the former Soviet Union outside the Baltic republics started on 2 January 1992, with the liberalisation of most retail and wholesale prices in Russia. An exception was made for the prices of the goods that played an important role in income redistribution mentioned above. Price liberalisation was achieved with the stroke of a pen. It requires only the passive government policy of *not* doing something, i.e. not controlling prices or convertibility. This is an important difference between liberalisation on the one hand and stabilisation and privatisation on the other. Once inflation and state property exist, they do not disappear overnight; but fixed prices can disappear overnight. This difference has been decisive in the solution of the largely academic 'sequencing' debate. In the end, all ex-Communist states started their transition with at least a partial price liberalisation because this could be achieved most quickly.

In the Russian Federation those prices that were kept fixed at first were gradually liberalised later. For example, the price of crude oil, 0.4 per cent of the world market price in December 1991, was increased administratively a few times before being liberalised formally in September 1992 (CER 1993a: 26). After that it remained much lower than the world market price for crude oil; the markets were separated via export quotas. As these quotas were also gradually reduced, the price of crude oil rose to 50–60 per cent of world market levels in 1995. Similarly, the government officially stopped procuring grain from farmers at above market-level prices in September 1993 (CER 1993b: 29). In the summer of 1993, the government grain procurement price exceeded the market price by 40 per cent (Åslund 1995: 165). In 1992, subsidies to agriculture still amounted to 7.7 per cent of GNP (Åslund 1995: 164). This phenomenon serves to demonstrate that the different elements of a transition policy are related. The lack of liberalisation in the agricultural sector led to huge state expenses, increasing the budget deficit and hence hampering stabilisation.

An interesting lesson of price liberalisation in the Russian Federation is that it is easier to do away with price controls than with the committee responsible for them. Gostsen, the price-setting comittee of the former USSR, continued to exist and to lobby for the reintroduction of fixed prices. It almost succeeded in December 1992 (Åslund 1995: 144).

To avoid a complete sell-out of tradables, all ex-USSR republics had to follow the initial price liberalisation of January 1992 to some extent. However, alternative measures were adopted as well. In Ukraine, for example, part of the response to Russian price liberalisation consisted of imposing export barriers (Dabrowski 1994: 118). This enabled Ukraine to engage in more price control than Russia. Many republics followed a similar policy. As can be seen from Table 9.2, in 1994 five republics still used extensive price controls and state procurement.

The data in Table 9.2 may give rise to the idea that liberalisation has been a continuous process in the former Soviet Union, but this is not the case. For example, in the case of Ukraine many controls on the economy were reimposed towards the end of 1993, only to be abandoned again in 1994 and 1995 (Tedstrom 1995: 6). Similarly in Russia, the process of liberalisation was a struggle between reformers and interest groups; at times the former had the upper

121

Table 9.2 Liberalisation

	Price liberalisation		Trade and foreign exchange	
	1994	*1995*	*1994*	*1995*
Russia	3	3	3	3
Ukraine	2	3	1	3
Belarus	2	3	1	2
Uzbekistan	3	3	2	2
Kazakhstan	2	3	2	3
Georgia	2	3	1	2
Azerbaidzjan	3	3	1	2
Lithuania	3	3	4	4
Moldova	3	3	2	4
Latvia	3	3	4	4
Kirgizstan	3	3	3	4
Tadzjikistan	3	3	1	2
Armenia	3	3	2	3
Turkmenistan	2	2	1	1
Estonia	3	3	4	4

Source: EBRD (1994: 10) and EBRD (1995: 11)
Notes:
Price liberalisation:
2 = Price controls for several important product categories including energy; state procurement remains important.
3 = Substantial progress on price liberalisation including energy prices; state procurement largely phased out.

Trade and foreign exchange system:
1 = Widespread import and/or export controls or very limited legitimate access to foreign exchange.
2 = Some liberalisation of import and/or export controls; almost full current account convertibility in principle but possibly with multiple exchange rates.
3 = Removal of most quantitative and administrative import and export restrictions; almost full current account convertibility at a unified exchange rate.
4 = Removal of all quantitative and administrative import and export restrictions and all significant export tariffs.

hand, at times the latter (see Åslund 1995: chapter 5). The overall trend is, however, clearly towards increased liberalisation.

Thus we see that as in the case of stabilisation, the possibility of adopting different liberalisation strategies was widely used by the fifteen successor states. The differences are even more pronounced if we analyse the liberalisation of foreign trade and money. As Table 9.2 makes clear, external liberalisation entails abandoning export and import controls and current account convertibility at a unified exchange rate. By doing so, trade relations among decentralised agents (producers and consumers) in different countries are made possible. This increases the size of the market, a major factor in explaining *the wealth of nations* ever since Adam Smith's pin factory. Decentralised trade can then replace the Communists' method of increasing the size of the market (or the size of the plan?), i.e. state trade. This is important because various attempts to keep state trade alive since January 1992 have not been successful. For example, the oil-for-sugar deals between the governments of Russia and Cuba have turned out to be one of the old habits that die hard. They continued to be made but not to be implemented. This is no mystery, because the government's grip on the economy becomes much weaker as privatisation and liberalisation proceed (as they did in Russia but not in Cuba); hence it becomes harder to keep promises to other governments. In trade among the Newly Independent States, similar state deals were made, and similar problems arose in their implementation. As we discussed in the previous chapter, the fact that Russia on the whole succeeded better in keeping its promises than the other successor states resulted in a massive build-up of debts to Russia by the other successor states. Thus, a new trade mechanism is needed, a mechanism that is compatible with a market economy.

The potential benefits from trade are especially high for less developed countries, because open economies tend to converge, whereas closed economies do not (Sachs and Warner 1995: 3). Empirical evidence given by Sachs and Warner (1995: 42) shows that for open economies, economies that initially have a low GNP per capita grow faster than countries with a high GNP per capita. For closed economies this is not true (Sachs and Warner 1995: 43). This is attributed to the distribution of international knowledge via international trade. For the poor ex-USSR, this is an important additional reason to open up.

The pattern that arises from a comparison of the external liberalisation policies in the ex-USSR is like that of stabilisation and price liberalisation. The three Baltic states were the most energetic reformers; within the CIS, Russia took the lead. In July 1992 the rouble exchange rate was essentially unified and the rouble made convertible on the current account (Åslund 1995: 148). By 1995, almost full current account convertibility at a unified exchange rate had been achieved in nine of the fifteen ex-USSR republics. The exchange rate regimes within the group of nine were, however, quite diverse, ranging from the Estonian currency board via the Russian target zone to the Ukrainian float. Turkmenistan, the laggard in Table 9.2, unified its exchange rate in April 1996. With a few nuances, the same pattern of leaders and laggards can also be traced in the progress made in privatisation.

PRIVATISATION

The need for privatisation as an element of a transition strategy also follows immediately from a comparison between Communism and capitalism. In a market economy most enterprises are private, whereas in a Communist economy they are state owned. Hence the state-owned enterprises must be privatised. There is, however, an alternative to privatisation: entry. As the case of Poland shows, it is quite possible to arrive at a predominantly private economy without the large-scale privatisation of industrial enterprises. After more than six years of squabbling about the exact form that large-scale privatisation should take the Poles organised a referendum on the matter on 16 February 1996. It did not solve anything; the referendum was non-binding on account of the low turnout of voters. Nevertheless, in 1995 60 per cent of Polish GDP was already being produced by private enterprises (EBRD 1995: 11). The Polish case also highlights the disadvantages of this method, in that the economy will be stuck with a large state-owned sector for many years.

The importance of privatisation for achieving efficient economic outcomes has been demonstrated most innovatively and comprehensively in Boycko *et al.*'s *Privatizing Russia* (1995). Their analysis is based on a distinction between two types of property rights: control rights and cash flow rights. Applied to an enterprise, control rights involve the right to decide what an enterprise should produce, how many people it should employ, where it should locate, and so on. Cash flow rights are the rights to the proceeds of the enterprise. These property rights can be held by the state (bureaucrats), by the enterprise managers and workers (insiders), or by others (outsiders). 'Privatisation' is the transfer of cash flow rights from the state to insiders or outsiders; 'corporatisation' is the shift of control rights from the state to insiders or outsiders.

Why would it be important to transfer a certain type of property right from one group of owners to another? Because economic efficiency demands that either property rights be concentrated in a single hand, or an effective contract between the holders of different property rights operate. The reason why the Communist economies were performing so poorly is, according to the authors, that this condition was not fulfilled. Under Communism, all property rights were officially held by the state. In reality, however, property rights were divided among bureaucrats, managers and the public. Control rights were held mainly by state bureaucrats, and to some extent by enterprise managers. They took the decisions on what to produce, how to produce, etc. The consequences of these decisions were, however, not borne by managers and politicians, but by the public at large. They paid for politicians' and managers' decisions in terms of their living standards.

In the Soviet Union, the regime used its control rights over the economy to build a powerful state, with a huge army and police capable of defending the Communist government from the threats of both external invasion and internal unrest. Under Gorbachev, many control rights shifted from bureaucrats to managers, whereas the cash flow rights remained with the public. This did not improve efficiency. At that point, the managers rather than officialdom pursued their own goals; for example, by simply stealing enterprise assets. The core problem was that neither the managers nor the bureaucrats were entitled to (a portion of) the proceeds of their decisions.

Given this inheritance, what should reformers do? In a chapter entitled 'Paths to Efficient Ownership', Boycko *et al.* discuss a number of solutions. For example, in a situation where managers have cash flow rights (obtained via 'spontaneous privatisation', i.e. the illegal grabbing of cash flow rights by managers) and some control rights, and bureaucrats have some remaining control rights, the problem of divided property rights can be solved by a 'contract' between managers and bureaucrats. The managers pay the bureaucrats not to use their control rights. This phenomenon is known as corruption. 'Corruption' is discussed here without any of the moral stigma usually associated with the term. The problem with corruption, however, is that corruption contracts are not enforceable in court. In this example of a particular model of property rights, contracting cannot reduce the inefficiencies.

Through analyses of different types of property rights models, the authors make clear that the problem can be solved only by the combination of corporatisation and privatisation. Property rights must be depoliticised, because when enterprises are subject to

125

political influence, they cater to the political brass by producing goods that consumers do not want, employing too many people, etc. Corporatisation and privatisation force enterprises to cater to consumers and shareholders.

In the booming literature on privatisation in Eastern Europe, many other goals and subgoals of privatisation are mentioned by various authors, such as raising state revenue, attracting foreign investment, increasing social justice, and the need to privatise with some speed (see, for example, the various contributions in Smit and Pechota 1994). The main competing thesis, however, is the view that the prime goal of privatisation is not to combat political discretion, but rather managerial discretion. It is claimed that there may be some advantage in the sense of decreasing the possibility of abuse of political power, but that the chief purpose is to create a sound regime of corporate governance (Smit and Pechota 1994: 61). In such a scenario, it is especially important to create outside ownership that is concentrated enough to control management effectively.

The different goals of privatisation can clash and hence priorities must be set. The choice of the main aim(s) of privatisation is closely related to the choice of the method of privatisation. If attracting foreign capital is deemed paramount, a case-by-case sale to foreigners may seem the best option. This was tried, for example, in Kazakhstan. Speedy depoliticisation is best served by a voucher approach, as the experience in Russia and the Czech Republic teaches us. If corporate governance is the privatisers' main concern, something like the Polish 'mutual funds' plan might be adopted. In this plan, each citizen was slated to obtain a share in each of some twenty National Investment Funds. Each fund would then receive the controlling share of some twenty medium or large enterprises (Smit and Pechota 1994: 180). Thus, ownership rights would be concentrated in the mutual funds, and mutual funds would therefore have an incentive to control the managers of the enterprises in their portfolio. As we have noticed, however, progress in Polish privatisation has thus far been extremely slow. Boycko *et al.* (1995: 13) argue that this is due to the fact that the Poles concentrated on the wrong problem.

Learning from the experience of their neighbours to the west, the Russian privatisers decided to follow a road similar to that taken by the Czech Republic. In the Czech privatisation of med- ium- and large-scale enterprises, an important role was played by non-tradable and registered vouchers, denominated in points (each voucher was worth 1,000 points). These were handed out to the population for a fee of 1,035 Czech crowns, equal to approximately 25 per cent of the average monthly wage. Subsequently, these vouchers could be used either to buy shares in centralised auctions, or to invest in an investment fund. With the points, an individual or a fund could file a bid for shares in a certain enterprise. In the first round, all shares had the same price, namely 33 points. After the bids were made, in the case of excess supply, demand was satisfied, and the remaining shares were put up in the next round for a price lower than 33 points. In the case of excess demand, no shares were awarded, and the shares were offered at a higher price in the next round. Frydman *et al.* (1993: 85) call this procedure 'discrete time *tatonnement*'. The procedure sounds a bit roundabout, but it functioned fairly well in practice. Moreover, as investment funds came to dominate the privatisation process, excessive dispersal of property rights was avoided, so that the goal of policing corporate governance was also achieved. The system was speedy and allowed all Czechs a chance to participate. The primary goals of privatisation were thus met (Smit and Pechota 1994: 201).

Except for a few noteworthy differences, the Russian privatisers adopted the Czech approach. Unlike Czech vouchers, Russian vouchers were denominated in money terms, tradable and non-registered, and the auction mechanism was much simpler. No attempt was made to sell all enterprises at the same time or to value the enterprises. Instead, enterprises were auctioned one by one, and simply by dividing the number of shares up for auction (usually 29 per cent of total shares) by the number of vouchers handed in. The valuation problem was thus avoided. The vouchers were much cheaper than in the Czech Republic, and hence a lot more people collected them. By denominating the vouchers in money terms, a clear impression of a gift from the government to the people was conveyed. By allowing secondary trading and hence a market price for the vouchers, a sort of reform barometer was created. From the original nominal value of 10,000 roubles, the price first went down to 5,000 roubles but subsequently climbed to 40,000 roubles as privatisation in Russia gained momentum.

As in the Czech Republic, voucher privatisation was a great success in Russia. Speedy depoliticisation was achieved, and investment funds sprang up spontaneously, thus avoiding overly high dispersal of shares. The problem with Russian mass privatisation is, however, that in order to gain the support of managers and workers, these groups were given a huge proportion of the shares, in most enterprises 51 per cent. Contrary to what happened in the Czech Republic, in Russia property rights were, to a large extent, given to insiders and only to a smaller extent to outsiders. Thus, managerial discretion may remain a problem. However, with depoliticisation as the main goal of privatisation, this was a strategy that made sense.

Following the success of the Russian large-scale voucher priva-

Table 9.3 Progress in privatisation

	Large-scale privatisation		*Small-scale privatisation*	
	1994	*1995*	*1994*	*1995*
Russia	3	3	3	4
Ukraine	1	2	2	2
Belarus	2	2	2	2
Uzbekistan	2	3	3	3
Kazakhstan	2	2	2	2
Georgia	1	2	2	3
Azerbaidzjan	1	1	1	1
Lithuania	3	3	4	4
Moldova	2	3	2	3
Latvia	2	2	3	4
Kirgizstan	3	4	4	4
Tadzijikistan	2	2	2	2
Armenia	1	2	3	3
Turkmenistan	1	1	1	1
Estonia	3	4	4	4

Source: EBRD (1994: 10) and EBRD (1995: 11)
Notes:
For large-scale privatisation:
4 = More than 50 per cent of state-owned enterprises privatised in a scheme that has generated substantial outsider ownership.
3 = More than 25 per cent of large-scale enterprise assets privatised or in the process of being sold, but possibly with major unresolved issues regarding corporate governance
2 = Comprehensive scheme almost ready for implementation; some sales completed.
1 = Little progress.

For small-scale privatisation:
4 = Complete privatisation of small companies with tradable ownership rights.
3 = Nearly comprehensive programme implemented, but design or lack of government supervision leaves important issues unresolved.
2 = Substantial share privatised.
1 = Little progress.

tisation, other successor states have set up similar schemes. In Ukraine, for example, little progress was made in privatisation initially. By the end of 1993 only three industrial enterprises were privately owned (Kaser 1995: 148). A voucher-based mass privatisation programme slowly gained in strength. By 1996, 40 per cent of the population had collected their vouchers. Some 1,800 medium- to large-scale entreprises were offered for sale in voucher auctions in 1995, of which 600 have now been fully privatised (EBRD 1996: 9).

Table 9.3 makes clear that small-scale privatisation was generally easier to achieve than large-scale privatisation. Russia followed the example set in Eastern Europe by instructing local authorities to sell small enterprises for money at an auction (Åslund 1995: 248). We see in this table again the by now familiar pattern of economic reform in the Newly Independent States, with the Baltic republics in the vanguard, followed by Russia as one of the champions of reform in the CIS. No progress at all in privatisation was made in Turkmenistan and Azerbaidzjan, according to this EBRD classification.

CONCLUSION

We can summarise the results obtained as follows. On all indicators, the three Baltic republics have done better than the CIS countries. Within the CIS, Russia is a relatively quick reformer. It has stabilised, liberalised and privatised more actively than countries such as Ukraine and especially Turkmenistan, the republic that did least to establish a market economy. In discussing the importance of stabilisation, liberalisation and privatisation, various reasons have been given for why these elements of a transition policy are important for economic performance in theory. In the final analysis, however, the proof of the pudding is in the eating, and better policies should lead to higher economic growth. Better transition strategies would lead us to expect that the economic performance of the Baltic republics should outdo that of the CIS states, and that within the CIS the performance of Russia should outdo that of most other Newly Independent States. The evidence seems by and large to support this thesis. As we saw in Table 2.3, in 1995 the only countries experiencing growth after the post-transitional recession were the three Baltic republics plus Armenia. The recession in Russia seemed to be bottoming out, whereas some notoriously slow reformers such as Belarus, Tadzjikistan and Azerbaidzjan were still experiencing steep declines in GNP. On the basis of the evidence available, it seems that reforms pay off.

Two exceptions to this general trend can be used to make clear that other forces are also at work. Together with the three Baltic republics, Armenia was the only ex-USSR republic that experienced economic growth in 1995, even though its reform record is only mediocre. On the other hand, Kirgizstan's post-communist recession still continued in 1995, even though its reform record was comparable to that of the Baltic republics and better than Russia's on most indicators. We would expect Kirgizstan at some point to start reaping the benefits of its active reform policy.

To summarise, in the case of the former Soviet Union the possibility of designing one's own transition strategy has been an important economic effect of political break-up. The possibility of developing a transition strategy has proved to be an economic benefit of Soviet break-up for Estonia, Latvia and Lithuania. On the other hand, for some other successor states discretion turned out to be worse than rules. The economic performance of Belarus or Azerbaidzjan would probably have been better today if they had been forced to follow Moscow's economic reforms after 1992.

10

CONCLUSION

Economic relations among ex-USSR republics: past, present and future

INTRODUCTION

In this book we have analysed economic relations among the republics of the former Soviet Union. As we have seen in Chapters 4 and 5, in the past the Soviet Union was a highly integrated economic space. The individual republics were extremely open and cooperated above all with each other. A uniform and centralised planning system fulfilled the task of coordinating economic activity and trade flows, evidently with some success. The political disintegration of the Soviet Union and the transformation of the economic order from a planned to a market economy produced a double threat to existing economic integration: 1   political borders need not, but mostly do, increase transaction costs and hence reduce the scope for mutually beneficial trade; 2   the sudden collapse of the central planning system and the only gradual emergence of a market price mechanism create a chaotic interlude in which cooperation will be reduced to a minimum. (Wagener and van Selm 1993: 421)

PAST

In the days of the Union economic cooperation among the republics was imperative. In the 1977 constitution of the USSR, art.16 stipulated that the republics are part of a 'Unified National Economic Entity'. Contrary to other articles in the Soviet constitution (see Chapter 3), this was not a dead letter. The economy of the USSR was planned from Moscow on a sectoral, not a regional, basis. Gosplan (the state planning committee) issued its orders to the (sectoral) ministries in Moscow, and these ministries in turn supervised most of the enterprises.

131

This economic command structure was disrupted under Khrushchev. As part of an economic and political reform strategy, Khrushchev switched from a ministerial to a territorial scheme of planning organisations. Under the ministerial rule of central planning, trade was planned centrally with a certain ministerial bias (*vedomstvennost*) in order to keep shortage goods within the domain of the ministry. Under the territorial rule of central planning, trade was planned cooperatively by central and regional authorities with a strong regional bias (*mestnichestvo*) in order to keep shortage goods within the boundaries of the region: that is, loosening the strict hierarchical control made the USSR fall apart, even under Communism (Wagener and van Selm 1993: 414).

In the original plans put forward in 1957, there were 105 local economic councils or *sovnarkhozy*. Of these, seventy were in Russia, nine in Kazakhstan, eleven in Ukraine and four in Uzbekistan; the other eleven republics were co-extensive with a *sovnarkhoz* (Nove 1989: 337). But this arrangement produced mainly confusion, and Khrushchev's successors quickly abandoned it. The sector orientation dominated over most of Soviet history, and this explains the important interdependencies among the economies of the fifteen Newly Independent States. The situation would have been very different today if Khrushchev's reforms had lasted.

Also under Khrushchev, large development projects in peripheral republics were started, and capital was redistributed on a large scale from the three Slavic republics to the peripheral Central Asian republics. The redistribution in favour of Kazakhstan began in connection with the Virgin Lands Campaign in March 1954. The share of Uzbekistan in Soviet investment experienced a two-fold increase during the 1960s. The 'rich-to-poor' pattern of capital transfers was continued until the late 1970s, as we have seen in Chapter 8. In the 1980s, capital transfers were still very substantial, but the pattern of transfers was less clear. In Chapter 2, we pointed out that one of the main economic effects of the break-up of the Soviet Union into fifteen independent states is that these redistribution flows will come to an end.

PRESENT

The disintegration of the 'Unified National Economic Entity' as it is currently taking place is best illustrated by the monetary disintegration of the USSR. In our analysis in Chapter 1, we made it clear that a major effect of political break-up is that the former Soviet republics are no longer automatically in a Monetary Union. In the days of the Union all republics used the Soviet rouble depicting Lenin, as well as bank account roubles. The Lenin roubles were used on the labour and consumer markets. In exchange between enterprises, bank accounts denominated in roubles were used. A typical trait of the Soviet economic system was that these bank roubles were inconvertible or only partly convertible to cash roubles.

In January 1992, the Central Bank of Russia opened correspondent accounts for all former Soviet republics. These accounts replaced the interbranch payments mechanism used by Gosbank, the state bank of the USSR, under the system of central planning. In Soviet days, each branch had a correspondent account with Gosbank, so that it was always possible to know whether a given *branch* was in deficit or in surplus with the rest of Gosbank (IMF 1994: 33). But it was impossible to see whether a given *republic* was in surplus or deficit with Gosbank, so therefore a change was necessary. In the first half year following the introduction of the correspondent accounts their use was limited to observation. Cash was, however, controlled in Moscow, and tightly so. This induced various republics to circulate coupons along with old rouble notes and bank roubles (Granville 1994: 8).

Russia thus had a monopoly in the creation of cash roubles, but not in the creation of substitutes for it or in the creation of bank account roubles. As we have seen in Chapter 6, in this situation the incentives to create money were strong, because the benefits accrued only to the spending republic, whereas the costs (increased inflation) spread over the whole area. To put an end to this situation, republican bank account roubles were made inconvertible to Russian account roubles in July 1992. One year later, central bank president Gerashchenko defended his monetary reform as an attempt to do the same for cash roubles. Indeed, for Georgia, Turkmenistan, Azerbaidzjan and Moldova, the events of July 1993 were reason to leave or speed up leaving the rouble zone (Ukraine, Estonia, Latvia, Lithuania and Kirgizstan had already left the rouble zone). The remaining republics followed in November 1993, with the exception of only Tadzjikistan, which introduced its own currency in March 1995.

In each case of a republic leaving the rouble zone, agreements were signed with Russia regarding the suspension or repatriation of roubles, but to date no repatriation has taken place. In Ukraine, only around 0.1 per cent of the rouble issue was recovered. Kirgizstan did better here and recovered 27 per cent (IMF 1994: 43). The issue of the non-repatriation of roubles continues to play a role in the relations among the successor states. In April 1996, the Russian government requested compensation from Estonia for non-returned roubles amounting to $170 million, equal to the value of 2.6 billion roubles in June 1992 (OMRI 9 April 1996). In reply, the Estonians pointed out that the losses related to half a century of enforced Communism were much greater.

'Real' disintegration has also been rapid. Trade among the republics has been hampered by limitations on exports and by the continued dominance of state trading organisations (Michalopoulos and Tarr 1994: 1). Export taxes were raised to produce government revenue and to slow the adjustment to world market prices. Even though central planning had ceased, Russian ministries continued to perform 'material balance' calculations through 1993 to determine the residual above domestic 'needs' that could be exported (Michalopoulos and Tarr 1994: 9). As a result of such policies, trade among the republics declined by at least 65 per cent over the years 1990–3 (Michalopoulos and Tarr 1994: 3).

FUTURE

As the rouble area was unravelling, various economic and monetary treaties were signed among various subgroups of the Newly Independent States. In this book we have argued against the creation of a former Soviet Customs Union (Chapter 6), Monetary Union (Chapter 6) and Payments Union (Chapter 7) on the basis of economic theory. Nevertheless, all three kinds of unions have been agreed upon by subgroups. To present just a few examples, ten CIS states decided to form a Payments Union in Bishkek on 9 October 1992; an agreement to revive a rouble zone was signed by Russia, Kazakhstan, Uzbekistan, Tadzjikistan, Belarus and Armenia on 7 September 1993; two weeks later a treaty on 'economic cooperation' (the progressive establishment of first a free trade zone, then a Customs Union, and finally a Common Market) was signed by the same republics plus Kirgizstan, Moldova and Azerbaidzjan, whereas reportedly Turkmenistan is an 'associate member' to this treaty and Ukraine a 'provisional associate member' (IMF 1994: 8); Russia and Belarus signed a treaty to form a

Monetary Union on 12 April 1994; at a conference in Almaty on 8 July 1994, Kazakhstan, Kirgizstan and Uzbekistan signed a treaty to form an Economic and Defence Union; in March 1996, Russia, Belarus, Kazakhstan and Kirgizstan signed a 'Treaty on Deepening Integration in Economic and Humanitarian Spheres' including a common goods market (OMRI 1 April 1996); and in April 1996, Russia and Belarus signed a 'Treaty on Forming a Community' that according to Russian central bank chairman Dubinin implies a fixed exchange rate system between the two roubles like the European Monetary System (OMRI 6 April 1996), and according to deputy chairman Pokrovski, of the Interstate Economic Committee a 'payments union and a common currency' (OMRI 3 May 1996) between Russia and Belarus.

Thus far none of these treaties has had much practical meaning. There is a huge gap between signing a piece of paper after a long day of meetings and really doing something. It is my contention that without political reintegration such treaties among sovereign states will remain dead letters. Also, these forms of integration are unnecessary. The republics should simply adopt the right economic policy at home (as some already have, see Chapter 9), and then economic cooperation will follow automatically and spontaneously. For example, if all the republics adopt a convertible currency there is no need for a Payments Union. Moreover, as we have seen in the case of West European integration in Chapter 6, the additional benefits of having a Monetary Union over having convertible currencies are small.

If a meaningful institutional integration form is to be created in the former Soviet Union, it can be only after renewed political integration. This is, in my opinion, a very real possibility. Many Russian politicians would push for an *Anschluß* of at least Ukraine and Belarus if in power. This option would make everybody worse off, from an economic as well as from any other point of view. Let us hope that *The Economics of Soviet Return* will never be written.

THE SIZE OF THE PIE AND ITS DISTRIBUTION REVISITED

The hypothesis that we derived from the analysis of the 'Border Irrelevance Proposition' was that the combined GNP of the constituent parts that formed a state before break-up (the 'size of the pie') probably decreases on account of the break-up, because the

135

negative effects are more numerous than the positive effects (even though we did not attempt to establish the relative weight of the different effects). Moreover, we identified two factors that bear on the 'distribution of the pie', i.e. the relative performance of the successor states: redistribution and economic reform. We should be able to explain some of the relative performance in GNP on account of these two factors.

The data on GNP in Eastern Europe available in spring 1996 allow for some empirical 'testing' of these hypotheses. The fact that the combined GNP of the USSR successor states has been halved since January 1992 seems to support the first hypothesis. The size of the pie has definitely decreased, but has it decreased because of the break-up or because of the transition recession? Other ex-Communist states in Eastern Europe that did not break up also experienced huge GNP declines. The argument then rests on the fact that the cumulative post-Communist decline in GNP has been much more substantial in the ex-USSR than in Poland, Hungary, Romania or Bulgaria. In Eastern Europe, cumulative GNP decline from 1989 to 1994 in states which did not break up ranged from Poland's 8.7 per cent to Bulgaria's 26.4 per cent; by 1994, all economies were growing again (EBRD 1995: 182). In the former Soviet Union, however, the unweighted average decline in GNP over the period 1989–95 was 52.1 per cent, ranging from Uzbekistan's 18 per cent to Georgia's 83 per cent. All economies except the three Baltic economies were still in decline in 1995.

This difference between the economic performance of Eastern Europe on the one hand and the former Soviet Union on the other is of course partly caused by situations of conflict in four ex-USSR republics: Armenia, Azerbaidzjan, Georgia and Tadzjikistan. These four republics experienced the biggest cumulative declines in GNP, with 63 per cent, 65 per cent, 83 per cent and 60 per cent respectively (EBRD 1995: 185). However, if we exclude these four republics and take the unweighted average decline in GNP of only the other eleven republics, the drop is still 46.4 per cent, much more than in the 'non-breaking' states of Eastern Europe. From this evidence one might be tempted to conclude that the difference is caused by break-up.

However, the evidence is too meagre to justify the conclusion that break-up reduces the size of the pie. The USSR is but a single case. Comparing developments in the GNP of the former Soviet Union to developments in GNP elsewhere in Eastern Europe immediately leads us to a falsification of the hypothesis that break-up reduces the size of the pie: namely, Czechoslovakia. The break-up of this state also had many economic effects. Separate currencies were introduced and the common budget disappeared. In the first year after the break-up, trade between the Czech Republic and the Slovak Republic declined by 20 per cent (Dedek *et al.* 1996: 170). GNP in the Czech Republic and in the Slovak Republic declined, but the two states performed better than other East European states that did not break up, such as Bulgaria and Romania. The reason for this is probably that ex-Czechoslovakia was more successful at stabilising, liberalising and privatising than Romania or Bulgaria. The latter two experienced higher inflation and less liberalisation and privatisation than the two Czechoslovak successor states (EBRD 1994: 10; 1995: 11; 1996: 22). In economies in transition, the reform strategy chosen has such a strong effect on GNP that other relevant factors disappear from view. Breaking states that are in a transition from a planned economy to a market economy are therefore not ideal test cases for the hypothesis that break-up reduces the size of the pie.

What about the distribution of the pie? In the previous chapter, we found that differences in economic reform strategies can, to a considerable extent, explain differences in economic performance in the Newly Independent States. On the whole, the republics that stabilised, liberalised and privatised their economies are now experiencing economic growth, whereas those who did not are still in decline. Therefore the ability to develop different reform strategies has been one of the main economic effects of political break-up. This confirms part of the second hypothesis.

The other factor that bears on the relative performance of the successor states is the fact that redistribution via a common budget disappears. However, as we saw in Chapter 8, redistribution continued after December 1991 via a number of different channels. In Chapter 4, we concluded that the end of redistribution would benefit Russia and harm all other republics (except Turkmenistan). However, redistribution did not come to a halt. Therefore it is not really surprising that Russia is not performing better than could have been expected on the basis of its relative success at reforming its economy.

BORDER RELEVANCE

Comparing past, present and future economic relations among ex-USSR republics leads us to the final conclusion of this study, which is that the USSR case shows that political borders can be extremely relevant economically. The question *Do borders matter?* can be answered by a clear *Yes*. Today economic performance in the Soviet successor states is widely divergent. The dominant economic effect of political break-up has been the possibility to develop one's own transition strategy. This is an interesting result, because the role of the state as a system elector or as a designer of a transition strategy is not even mentioned in the precious little theorising that exists on the question *Do borders matter?*

In Chapter 2, we have drawn up a checklist on the economic effects of a political border. This list is far from the last word on the matter, but it is a huge improvement over the existing body of knowledge on the subject. Surprisingly, economic theory on the relevance of political borders is in its infancy. By studying the wealth of *nations* instead of continents, cultures or individuals, Smith put economics on the right track, but the follow-up to this has been infinitesimal.

What does exist is Nordhaus *et al.*'s 'Border Irrelevance Proposition'. We have scrutinised this proposition in Chapter 2, and we have shown that it is not particularly good. Still it is better than nothing. The existence of a field of economics called *international economics* suggests that economic interaction between countries differs from economic interaction among parts of a country. Any handbook on international economics should start with the question *What is a country?* In the 1994 edition of Krugman and Obstfeld's handbook we do in fact find a section on this, but in the two earlier editions, as well as in all other handbooks on international economics, this basic question is absent. In Krugman and Obstfeld's (1994, and the question only pops up on page 174!) book, four reasons are given for why borders matter from an economic point of view:

1 Political borders can be barriers to trade.
2 There can be differences in national currencies.
3 Regulations and standards can differ.
4 Labour mobility among countries may not be free.

The present account makes clear that this list is far from exhaustive. Even if all of these four conditions are fulfilled, borders can still be very significant from an economic point of view. Let us illustrate this by looking at the integration process in Western Europe. The 1957 Treaty of Rome guaranteed free trade and free labour mobility, the 1992 campaign has standardised the different European regulations, and if 1999 succeeds there will be a single European currency. Hence, by the year 1999, all of the Krugman and Obstfeld conditions may be fulfilled. Does this mean that intra-European borders will no longer be economically significant? No! For example, Krugman and Obstfeld's list leaves out one of the most important economic aspects of a state, which is the right to raise taxes. Only a very small portion of this prerogative has been transferred to Brussels thus far. Currently, the EU budget amounts to 1.2 per cent of the EU GDP. This fraction is set to rise to about 1.3 per cent by the year 2000 (Baldwin 1994: 170). Conversely, states often have budgets as large as 50 per cent of GNP. Because of this, income redistribution among the regions of a state is often huge. In Western Europe in 1999, even if there is a full Monetary Union, there will be redistribution within states from rich to poor regions, but little redistribution from rich to poor member states.

It may sound a little easy and commonplace to round off a study by declaring that 'much more research is needed', but it is my contention that in the case of the economic relevance of political boundaries this is wholly justified. The question is important but little studied. The EU example shows that borders need not be very important from an economic point of view, even though the economic aspects of political borders are manifold. The subject of this study, the Soviet case, shows that the economic effects of political break-up can be huge.

NOTES

4 FORMER SOVIET REPUBLICS' ECONOMIC INTERDEPENDENCE

1 As with Goskomstat (1990a) and Marer (1985), we use the expression 'valuta rouble' for the quantity of roubles that is obtained by applying the official dollar/rouble exchange rate to a quantity of dollars. Others use the term 'transferable rouble' (TR) for this (Clement 1990; Lavigne 1985), but it seems preferable to use TRs only with respect to intra-CMEA trade.

2 Marer (1985: 39) states that it is likely that the method employed by the Soviets to calculate PPP contains both upward and downward biases that cancel each other out at least to some extent. Clement (1990: 21), however, uses an exchange rate of 1 TR = 1.6 roubles, because this is the exchange rate that was used in the late 1980s to make intra-CMEA 'non-commercial' transactions (tourism, for example) comparable to intra-CMEA goods exchange.

3 Goskomstat (1990a: 36; 1991: 16) data on 'the specific weight of exports in production' and 'the specific weight of imports in use' are of an entirely different nature, because the denominator is not a value-added measure. As no separate data on the numerator and the denominator are presented, these ratios cannot be easily converted into trade to GNP ratios. We must proceed differently.

4 See Marer (1985: 15) on this: 'the best practical method is the scaling up from official NMP on the basis of country-specific data'.

5 In Soviet statistics, we find the Union GNP/NMP ratio increasing from 1.34 in 1985, 1.38 in 1987 and 1.39 in 1988 to 1.41 in 1989; the reason for this trend could be either real growth in the Soviet economy or wishful Goskomstat thinking. See Goskomstat (1990c: 11–12).

6 In principle, financial flows could be analysed as well to assess these capital flows, but the data problems involved in this are enormous. Besides, the mixing up of financial flows and real flows should be avoided. For example, turnover taxes are relevant in a 'real' analysis only to the extent that they influence the price vector that is used to translate physical exchange into a 'trade' deficit or surplus; the total

140

amount of turnover taxes, or whether the republic is allowed to keep these taxes or should pay them into the state budget, is irrelevant. However, in a financial analysis, only the amount of the turnover taxes collected paid to the state budget is relevant.

7 According to Treml *et al.* (1972: 154), in equation (4.1) VRs are translated into roubles by multiplying by either the import conversion coefficient (in the case of a deficit) or the export conversion coefficient (in the case of a surplus). It is unclear whether this practice was still used in 1988.

8 The 'negative losses' implicit in Table 4.3 for Azerbaidzjan and Latvia are difficult to interpret but negligibly small.

9 The intra-USSR relative price of meat to oil (both in tons) was sixty-six in 1988 (derived from Miloserdov 1990: 58). Applying Goskomstat's recalculation factors would lead to a relative 'world market' price of 6.5. However, the relative price of meat to oil that can be derived from UN trade statistics is about thirty.

10 This is the kind of 'capital transfer' or 'subsidy' that was discussed by Marrese and Vanous (1983) and by Holzman in the context of intra-CMEA trade. It is important to note that this 'price subsidisation' was only a part of potential Soviet interrepublican 'subsidisation'. A Soviet republic could simply run a deficit on its 'balance of payments' without any financial consequences. A CMEA member's balance of payments had to be more or less in equilibrium; only implicit subsidies via prices were possible.

6 THE SOVIET UNION AS A CUSTOMS AND MONETARY UNION

1 Two other forms of integration, free trade areas and Common Markets, are referred to in the margin of this paper. The economics of free trade areas (i.e. Customs Unions without a common external tarriff) and Customs Unions are basically similar (but see El-Agraa (1982: 22) on some of the differences). A Common Market adds the free mobility of factors of production to the free mobility of goods. This form of integration is encountered in the case study of integration in Western Europe (the fourth section).

2 The term 'Monetary Union' should be reserved solely for a common currency and not be used in the case of fixed exchange rates. Breaking away from a fixed exchange rate area can occur at any time, whereas the introduction of a new currency takes time and effort.

3 If the parties concerned are too small to affect their terms of trade. See the literature on optimum tariffs, e.g. Krugman and Obstfeld (1991: 217).

4 List, (1922: 538ff.) used 'infant industry'-like arguments in defence of the German *Zollverein*. Conversely, the example of the aforementioned Methuen Treaty leads List to this generalization: *Schädliche illegitime Handelsverträge sind solche, wodurch eine bereits in der Entwicklung begriffene Manufakturkraft einer andern Nation zum Opfer gebracht wird* (p.73).

5 The words 'more likely' in Lipsey's proposition deserve some extra emphasis. Even if A trades a lot with B and little with C, a union with B can be harmful to A and a union with C can be beneficial. This depends on the magnitude of the price differences and the tariffs.

6 Shiller (in a reaction to Blanchard and Katz 1992: 71) argued that a priori one would expect capital mobility to be higher than labour mobility, because the value of residential housing stock depreciates slower than the value of venture capital. Hence, moving capital would normally be cheaper.

7 The 40 per cent is made up from an increase in federal grants of 6 per cent and a decrease in taxes paid of 34 per cent. Note, however, that von Hagen (1992: 344–5) has countered that this 40 per cent cannot be interpreted as a response to a transitory regional shock, but rather reflects the long-run redistributive properties of the system: 'The US fiscal system is designed to alleviate persisting inequalities, but does little to buffer transitory regional shocks'. Masson and Taylor (1993: 40) find results for Canada that bear out the conclusion of Sala-i-Martin and Sachs, i.e. that fiscal redistribution is important as an adjustment mechanism in Monetary Unions.

8 However, the *effectiveness* of fiscal policy might be increased by entry in a Monetary Union, as is suggested by the well-known Mundell–Fleming model. In this framework, with flexible exchange rates, monetary policy is effective, whereas fiscal policy is not; under fixed exchange rates, these results are reversed. Of course, entering a Monetary Union entails the fixing of the exchange rate with a part of the outside world.

9 A more sophisticated indicator for the likelihood of asymmetric shocks can be found in Gros and Thygesen (1992: 257–8). Their conclusion is the same: the least developed member states have most to lose from monetary unification because their economic structure differs most from the EC average.

10 In 1991 Germany, France, the UK and Luxemburg satisfied both fiscal criteria, i.e. a debt–GDP ratio of less than 60 per cent and a deficit–GDP ratio of less than 3 per cent. In 1992, only France and Luxemburg passed the test. See Buiter *et al.* (1993: 64–5).

11 This was later denied by IMF officials. For example, 'Contrary to a widespread myth, the Fund has never opposed the introduction of national currencies in the FSU' (Hernandez-Cata 1993: 54).

12 The literature on Soviet disintegration abounds with misinterpretations of Customs Union analysis. For example, in a recent World Bank publication, Michalopoulos and Tarr (1994) argue that 'preferential trade areas are intended to provide an incentive to the importer to buy the produce within the region of preference', i.e. Customs Unions are intended to lead to trade diversion! Economists can only hope that politicians have better intentions when they create Customs Unions.

8 THE SOVIET UNION AS A REDISTRIBUTOR

1 EU unrequited transfer data can be found in Swann (1988: 77). Imbalances in goods exchange can be calculated using Eurostat statistics.

2 However, during the short-lived experiment with regional economic councils (*Sovnarkhozy*) under Khrushchev, the economy was organised regionally first and sectorally only subsequently.

3 The potential conflict of 'intent' and 'effect' with respect to capital allocation is highlighted in Schiffer (1989: 10, 231ff.).

4 A translation of the standard Soviet formulation of this location rule contains the 'principle of specialisation and complex development' with respect to regional development. The aims of specialisation and complex development appear to conflict: the former seems to be aiming at output maximisation whereas the latter seems to be equality oriented. One may dismiss the principle, referring to the apparent contradiction as dialectic humbug. However, Dyker (1983: 115) seems to have found a way out in his formulation of the principle. Thus formulated, principle 3 may indeed serve both output maximisation and equality somewhat.

5 According to Schiffer (1989: 11), 'it is obvious to both Western specialists and Soviet scholars and politicians that the spatial decentralisation of industry in the USSR would not prevent the United States from destroying all of Soviet industrial power in the event of a nuclear war'.

6 The t-values are 2.082, 1.728 and 1.728 respectively. The critical value of t at the 95 per cent probability level is 1.771.

7 Glasnost produced a number of Soviet recalculations of economic growth; among these the Khanin recalculation is the most quoted. We took the Khanin data from Fisher (1992: 13).

8 Yet, the Central Asian republics remained receivers of capital over the whole range of our time series. The way out of this apparent contradiction is that the capital that flowed to the Central Asian republics was not invested, but rather consumed. According to Narzikulov (1992, annex 7), in Kirgizstan, Uzbekistan and Tadzhikistan in 1988 consumption alone was higher than national income!

9 Another explanation for the increased capital outflow from the Russian republic is presented by Burkett (1992: 163). He suggests that geo-political considerations that would supposedly benefit the RSFSR became less important in the second half of the 1980s.

10 Koropeckyj (1972: 73), Gillula (1979: 626), and Bond *et al.* (1990: 718). Wagener (1972: 8) assesses inequality between economic districts, *raiony*, of Tsarist Russia for 1908.

11 The fact that we use NIP instead of GDP has a diminishing effect on the observed level of inequality. The reason for this is that most services are not included in NIP, and more developed regions usually have a higher share of services in their national income.

12 The value of the coefficient of variation hovers around 0.16 up to 1983, and then rises steeply to 0.26 in 1991. The 'entropy' measure is

more or less stable at 0.05 up to 1983, and subsequently increased to 0.1 in 1991.

13 This danger threshold is reported by Havrylyshyn and Williamson (1991: 71). It would be reached even quicker if we were also to take the republics' share in Soviet foreign debt into account. In December 1991, an agreement among nine republics allocated some 61 per cent of Soviet debt to Russia, the remaining 39 per cent being shared by the others. In the course of 1992, however, various republics failed to make the required payments, and Russia had to take responsibility for 85 per cent of the debt. Estimates of Soviet hard currency debt range from $65 billion to $84 billion in 1991 (data from Planecon Report).

REFERENCES

AGIR (1994a), *The Interstate Bank: Genesis and Prospects for the Future*, Centre for Economic Policy Studies, Brussels.
—— (1994b), *AGIR Completion Report Nov 93–Jan 94*, Centre for Economic Policy Studies, Brussels.
—— (1994c), *Interim Report March–April 1994*, Centre for Economic Policy Studies, Brussels.
Allworth, E. ed. (1989), *Central Asia. 120 Years of Russian Rule*, Duke University Press, Duke, NC.
Arkadie, B. and M. Karlsson (1991), *Economic Survey of the Baltic Republics*, Study undertaken by the Swedish Ministry of Foreign Affairs, Stockholm.
Åslund, A. (1994), 'Lessons of the First Four Years of Systemic Change in Eastern Europe', *Journal of Comparative Economics*, vol. 19, no.1: 22–38.
—— (1995), *How Russia became a Market Economy*, Brookings Institution, Washington, DC.
Baldwin, R.E. (1994), *Towards an Integrated Europe*, CEPR, London.
Bayoumi, T. and B. Eichengreen (1992), 'Shocking Aspects of European Monetary Integration', *NBER Working Paper*, no.3949.
Bean, C.R. (1992), 'Economic and Monetary Union in Europe', *Journal of Economic Perspectives*, vol. 6, no.4: 31–53.
Belkindas, M.V. and M.J. Sagers (1990), 'A Preliminary Analysis of Economic Relations among Union Republics of the USSR; 1970–1988', in *Soviet Geography*, vol.31, no.9: 629–57.
Berg, G.P. van den (1991), *Soviet Recht en Staat in Beweging* (The Evolving Soviet Law and State), Ars Aequi Libri, Nijmegen.
Bergeyk, P.A.G. van and H. Oldersma (1990), 'Détente, Market-oriented Reform and German Unification: Potential Consequences for the World Trade System', *Kyklos*, no.4: 599-611.
Bergstrand, J.H. (1985), 'The Gravity Equation in International Trade: Some Microeconomic Foundations and Empirical Evidence', *The Review of Economics and Statistics*, vol.67: 474–81.
Biessen, G. (1991), 'Is the Impact of Central Planning on Foreign Trade Really Negative?', *Journal of Comparative Economics*, vol.15: 22–44.

145

REFERENCES

Blanchard, O.J. and L.F. Katz (1992), 'Regional Evolutions', *Brookings Papers on Economic Activity*, no.1: 175.

Bofinger, P. and D. Gros (1992), 'A Multilateral Payments Union for Eastern Europe: Why and How', *CEPR Discussion Paper* 654, Brussels.

Bolton, P. and G. Roland (1995), 'The Breakup of Nations: A Political Economy Analysis', *CEPR Working Paper*, no.1225.

Bond, A.R., M.V. Belkindas and A.I. Treyvish (1990), 'Economic Development Trends in the USSR, 1970–1988: Part 1', in *Soviet Geography*, vol.31, no.10: 705–31.

Boycko, M., A. Shleifer and R. Vishny (1995), *Privatising Russia*, MIT Press, Cambridge, MA.

Buiter, W., G. Corsetti and N. Roubini (1993), 'Excessive Deficits: Sense and Nonsense in the Treaty of Maastricht', *Economic Policy*, pp.58–100.

Burkett, J.P. (1992), 'Allocation of Investment among Soviet Republics in the 1980s', in M. Ellman and V. Kontorovich eds, *The Disintegration of the Soviet Economic System*, Routledge, London.

CEC (Commission of the European Communities) (1977), *Report of the Study Group on the Role of Public Finance in European Integration*, Brussels.

—— (1990a), 'One Market, One Money – an Evaluation of the Potential Benefits and Costs of forming an Economic and Monetary Union', *European Economy*, no.44.

—— (1990b), 'Stabilization, Liberalization and Devolution: Assessment of the Economic Situation and Reform Process in the Soviet Union', *European Economy*, no.45.

—— (1993), 'Shaping a Market-Economy Legal System. A Report of the EC/IS Joint Task Force on Law Reform in the Independent States', *European Economy Reports and Studies*, no.2.

CER (Centre for Economic Reforms), *Russian Economic Trends*, various issues.

Clement, H. (1990), 'Funktionsproblemen der Gemeinsame Währung des RWG (Transferabeler Ruble)', in H.J. Wagener ed., *Monetäre Steuerung und ihre Probleme in unterschiedlichen Wirtschaftssystemen*, Duncker & Humblot, Berlin, pp.187–213.

—— (1993), 'Zerfall und Neuaufbau der Arbeitsteilung zwischen den Republiken/Staaten', in *Wirtschaftsreformen in Mittel- und Osteuropa*, Berlin, pp.133–50.

Coase, R. (1960), 'The Problem of Social Cost', *Journal of Law and Economics*, pp.1–44.

Collins, S.M. and D. Rodrik (1991), 'Eastern Europe and the Soviet Union World Economy', *Institute for International Economics Policy Analyses* no.32.

Dabrowski, M. (1994), 'The Ukrainian Way to Hyperinflation', *Communist Economies and Economic Transformation*, no.2: 115–37.

Dedek, O. *et al.* (1996), *The Break-up of Czechoslovakia: An In-depth Economic Analysis*, Avebury, Aldershot.

Dehesa, G. de la and P. Krugman (1992), *EMU and the Regions*, Occasional Paper no. 39, Group of Thirty, Washington, DC.

Dornbusch, R. (1992), 'Monetary Problems of Post-Communism: Lessons from the End of the Austro-Hungarian Empire', *Weltwirtschaftliches Archiv*, vol.128: 391–423.

—— (1993), 'Payments Arrangements among the Republics', in O.

REFERENCES

Blanchard *et al.* eds, *Post Communist Reform. Pain and Progress*, MIT Press, Cambridge, MA, pp.81–108.

Dyker, D.A. (1983), *The Process of Investment in the USSR*, Cambridge University Press, Cambridge.

EBRD (1994), *Transition Report. Economic Transition in Eastern Europe and the Former Soviet Union*, London.

—— (1995), *Transition Report 1995. Investment and Enterprise Development*, London.

—— (1996), *Transition Report Update. April 1996*, London.

ECE (1993), *Economic Survey of Europe in 1992–93*, New York.

—— (1994), *Economic Bulletin for Europe*, New York.

Eichengreen, B. (1990), 'One Money for Europe? Lessons from the US Currency and Customs Union', *Economic Policy*, no.10: 117–87.

—— (1991), 'Is Europe an Optimum Currency Area?', *NBER Working Paper* no.3579.

—— (1993a), 'A Payments Union for the Former Soviet Union: Is the EPU a relevant precedent?', *Economic Policy*, no.17: 310–53.

—— (1993b), *Reconstructing Europe's Trade and Payments*, Manchester University Press, Manchester.

El-Agraa, A. (1982), 'The Theory of Economic Integration', in A. El-Agraa ed., *International Economic Integration*, St Martin's Press, New York, pp.10–28.

—— (1990), 'European Monetary Integration' in A. El-Agraa ed., *Economics of the European Community*, Philip Allen, Cambridge.

Ethier, W. (1985), *Modern International Economics*, W.W. Norton, New York.

Eurostat (1985), *Balance of Payments: Global data 1972–1983*, Brussels.

—— (1991), *Basic Statistics of the Community*, Brussels.

—— (1990), *Basic Statistics of the Community*, Brussels.

Fisher, S. (1992), 'Russia and the Soviet Union then and now', *NBER Working Paper*, no.4077.

—— (1993a), 'Socialist Economy Reform: Lessons of the first three years', *American Economic Review*, vol.83, no.2: 390–5.

—— (1993b), 'Comment', *Economic Policy*, no.17: 347–50.

Foroutan, F. (1993), 'Regional Integration in Sub-Saharan Africa', in J. De Melo and A. Panagariya eds, *New Dimensions in Regional Integration*, Cambridge University Press, Cambridge, pp.234–77.

Frydman, R., *et al.* (1993), *The Privatisation Process in Central Europe*, Central University Press, London.

Gaidar, E. (1995), *Russian Reform*, MIT Press, Cambridge, MA.

Garber, P.M. and M.G. Spencer (1994), 'The Dissolution of the Austro-Hungarian Empire: Lessons for Currency Reform', *Princeton Essays in International Finance*, no.191.

Gillula, J.W. (1979), 'The Economic Interdependence of Soviet Republics', in Joint Economic Committee, US Congress, *Soviet Economy in a Time of Change*, vol.1, Washington, DC, pp. 618–55.

Goskomstat SSSR (1988), *Material'no-technicheskoye obespecheniye narodnogo khozyaystva SSSR* (Material-technical Supply of the Economy of the USSR), Moscow.

—— (1989a), *Statisticheskiye materialy ob ekonomicheskom i sotsial'nom razvitii*

REFERENCES

soyuznykh i avtonomnykh respublik, avtonomykh oblastey i okrugov (Statistical Materials on the Economic and Social Development of Union and Autonomous Republics, Autonomous Oblasts and Okrugs), vol.1, Moscow.

Goskomstat SSSR (1989b), *Narodnoye Khozyaystvo SSSR v 1988 godu* (The National Economy in 1988), Moscow.

—— (1990a), 'Ekonomicheskiye vzaimosvyazi respublik v narodnokho-zyaystvennom komplekse (Economic Interrelations in the National Economic Complex), *Vestnik Statistiki,* no.3: 36–53.

—— (1990b), 'Ob'em vvoza i vyvoza produktsii po soyuznim respubli-kam za 1988 g. vo vnutrennikh i mirovykh tsenakh' (Volume of Imports and Exports of Soviet Republics in 1988 in Internal and World Prices), *Vestnik Statistiki,* no.4: 49–60.

—— (1990c), *Narodnoye Khozyaystvo SSSR v 1989 godu* (The National Economy of the USSR in 1989), Moscow.

—— (1991), *Socialniye razvitiye SSSR 1989. Staticheskii sbornik* (Social Development in the USSR. Statistical Manual), Moscow.

Granville, B. (1994), *So Farewell then Ruble Zone,* mimeo.

Grauwe, P. de (1992), 'German Monetary Unification', *European Economic Review,* vol.36: 435–45.

Greenaway, D. (1989), 'Regional Trading Arrangements and Intra-industry trade', in D. Greenaway, T. Hyclak and R. Thornton eds, *Economic Aspects of Regional Trading Arrangements,* Harvester Wheatsheaf, Exeter, pp.31–42.

Gros, D. (1994), *Intra CIS Payments. The Interstate Bank Project: Its Genesis and Demise,* mimeo.

Gros, D. and B. Dautrebande (1992), 'International Trade of Former Republics in the Long Run: An Analysis based on the "Gravity" Approach', *CEPS Working Document,* no.71, Brussels.

Gros, D. and A. Steinherr (1995), *Winds of Change. Economic Transition in Central and Eastern Europe,* Longman, London and New York.

Gros, D. and N. Thygesen (1992), *European Monetary Integration. From the European Monetary System to European Monetary Union,* Longman, London.

Hagen, J. von (1992), 'Fiscal Arrangements in Monetary Union: Evidence from the US', in *Fiscal Policy, Taxation and the Financial System in an Increasingly Integrated Europe,* Kluwer, Dordrecht, pp.337–59.

Hanson, P. (1990), 'The Baltic States. The economic and political implications of the secession of Estonia, Latvia and Lithuania from the USSR', *Special Report,* no.2033, The Economist Intelligence Unit, London.

Havrylyshyn, O. and J. Williamson (1991), *From Soviet Disunion to Eastern Economic Community?,* Institute for International Economics, Washington, DC.

Heleniak, T. (1995), 'Dramatic Population Trends in Countries of the FSU', *Transition. The Newsletter about Reforming Economies,* vol.6, no.9–10: 1–5.

Henderson, J. (1991), 'Legal Aspects of the Soviet Federal Structure', in A. McAuley ed., *Soviet Federalism. Nationalism and Economic Decentralisation,* Leicester University Press, Leicester, pp.33–55.

REFERENCES

Hernandez-Cata, E. (1993), 'The Introduction of National Currencies in the Former Soviet Union: Options, Policy Requirements and Early Experiences', in P. Bofinger ed., *The Economics of New Currencies*, CEPR, London.

Hirschman, A.O. (1980), *National Power and the Structure of Foreign Trade*, University of California Press, Berkeley, CA.

Holubnychy, V. (1973), 'Spatial Efficiency in the Soviet Economy', in V.N. Bandera and Z.L. Melnyk eds, *The Soviet Economy in Regional Perspective*, Praeger, New York, ch.1.

Holzman, F.D. (1987), *The Economics of Soviet Bloc Trade and Finance*, Westview Press, Boulder, CO.

Hunter, H. (1994), 'Transport in the Commonwealth of Independent States: An Aging Circulatory System', in Joint Economic Committee, US Congress, *The Former Soviet Union in Transition*, Washington, DC, pp. 597–609.

Illarionov, A. (1996), 'Finansovaya Stabilizatsia v Respublikakh Byfshevo SSSR' (Financial Stabilisation in the Republics of the Former USSR), *Voprosi Ekonomiki*, no.2: 64–87.

IMF (1992), *Common Issues and Interrepublic relations in the Former USSR*, Washington, DC.

—— (1993), *Economic Review: Ukraine*, Washington, DC.

—— (1994), *Financial Relations Among Countries of the Former Soviet Union*, Washington, DC.

Kaplan, J.J. and G. Schleiminger (1989), *The European Payments Union: Financial Diplomacy in the 1950s*, Clarendon, Oxford.

Kaser, M. (1995), 'Privatisation in the CIS', in A. Smith ed., *Challenges for Russian Economic Reform*, Royal Institute of International Affairs, London, pp.117–202.

Keynes, J.M. (1919), *The Economic Consequences of the Peace*, London.

Kindleberger, C.P. (1983), 'Standards as Public, Collective and Private Goods', *Kyklos*, pp. 377–96.

Koropeckyj, I.S. (1972), 'Equalization of Regional Development in Socialist Countries: An Empirical Study', *Economic Development and Cultural Change*, no.1: 68–86.

Kowalczyk, C. (1990), 'Welfare and Customs Union', *NBER Working Paper*, no.3476.

Krugman, P. (1987), 'Is Free Trade Passé?', *The Journal of Economic Perspectives*, vol.1, no.2: 131–44.

—— (1991), 'Increasing Returns and Economic Geography', *Journal of Political Economy*, vol.99: 483–99.

Krugman, P. and M. Obstfeld (1991), *International Economics. Theory and Policy*, 2nd edition, Harper Collins, New York.

—— (1994), *International Economics. Theory and Policy*, 4th edition, Harper Collins, New York.

Lange, O. (1936), 'On the Economic Theory of Socialism', *Review of Economic Studies*, no.1: 53–71.

Lavigne, M. (1985), *Economie Internationale des Pays Socialistes*, Colin, Paris.

Linnemann, H. (1966), *An Econometric Study of International Trade Flows*, North-Holland, Amsterdam.

REFERENCES

Lipsey, R.G. (1970), *The Theory of Customs Unions: A General Equilibrium Analysis*, Weidenfeld and Nicolson, London.

Lipton, D. and J.D. Sachs (1992), 'Prospects for Russia's Economic Reforms', *Brookings Papers on Economic Activity*, no.2, 213–83.

List, F. (1922), *Das Nationale System der Politischen Oekonomie. Der Internationale Handel, die Handelspolitik und der Deutsche Zollverein*, Jena (original 1841).

Marer, P. (1985), *Dollar GNPs of the USSR and Eastern Europe*, Johns Hopkins University Press, Baltimore, MD.

—— (1992), *Historically Planned Economies: A Guide to the Data*, World Bank Publications, Washington, DC.

Marrese, M. and Vanous, J. (1983), *Soviet Subsidization of Trade with Eastern Europe*, University of California Press, Berkeley, CA.

Masson, P.R. and M.P. Taylor (1993), 'Fiscal Policy within Common Currency Areas', *Journal of Common Market Studies*, no. 1: 29–44.

Mau, V. (1992), 'Comment', *Brookings Papers on Economic Activity*, no.2: 266–73.

McKinnon, R.I. (1963), 'Optimum Currency Areas', *American Economic Review*, vol. 53: 717–25.

Meade, J.E. (1957), 'The Balance of Payments Problems of a Free Trade Area', *Economic Journal*, vol. 47: 379–96.

Melitz, J. (1991), 'A Suggested Reformulation of the Theory of Optimal Currency Areas', *CEPR Discussion Paper Series*, no.590, October.

Mellor, R.E.H. (1988), *The Soviet Union and its Geographical Problems*, Macmillan, London.

Mencinger, J. (1994), 'The Birth and Childhood of a Currency: The Experience of Slovenia', in J. Gacs and G. Wickler eds, *International Trade and Restructuring in Eastern Europe*, Physica, Heidelberg.

Ménil, G. de and M. Maurel (1994), 'Breaking up a Customs Union: The Case of the Austro-Hungarian Empire in 1919', *Weltwirtschaftliches Archiv*, vol. 130: 553–75.

Michalopoulos, C. and D. Tarr (1992), *Trade and Payments Arrangements for States of the Former USSR*, World Bank Studies of Economies in Transformation, Washington DC.

—— eds (1994), *Trade in the New Independent States*, Studies of Economies in Transition no.13, World Bank, Washington, DC.

Miloserdov, V. (1990), 'Regionalniye khozyaystvenniye svyazi' (Regional Economic Relations), in *Planovoye Khozyaystvo* (Planned Economy), no.3: 57–66.

Mundell, R. (1961), 'A Theory of Optimal Currency Areas', *American Economic Review*, no.51: 657–65.

Narzikulov, R. (1992), 'Kyrgyzstan, Tadzhikistan, Turkmenistan, Uzbekistan', Paper presented at the conference on Economic Consequences of Soviet Disintegration, Vienna, 20–22 April.

Noble, J. and J. King (1991), *USSR. A Travel Survival Kit*, Lonely Planet, Berkeley, CA.

Nogués, J.J. and R. Quintanilla (1993), 'Latin America's Integration and the Multilateral Trading System', in J. De Melo, and A. Panagariya eds,

REFERENCES

New Dimensions in Regional Integration, Cambridge University Press, Cambridge, pp. 278–318.

Nordhaus, W.D., M.J. Peck and T.J. Richardson (1991), 'Do Borders Matter? Soviet Economic Reforms after the Coup', *Brookings Papers on Economic Activity*, no.2: 321–40.

Nove, A. (1989), *An Economic History of the USSR*, Pelican, London, 1989.

—— (1991), *The Economics of Feasible Socialism Revisited*, Harper Collins, London.

OMRI Daily Digest, various issues.

Pearson, R.P. (1991), 'The Historical Background to Soviet Federalism', in A. McAuley ed., *Soviet Federalism. Nationalism and Economic Decentralisation*, Leicester University Press, Leicester, pp. 13–32.

Pelkmans, J. (1984), *Market Integration in the European Community*, Nijhoff, The Hague.

Pomfret, R. (1986), 'The Theory of Preferential Trading Arrangements', *Weltwirtschaftliches Archiv* vol. 122: 439–99.

Robinson, E.A.G. ed. (1960), *The Economic Consequences of the Size of Nations*, Macmillan, London.

Robson, P. (1980), *The Economics of International Integration*, Allen and Unwin London.

Rosati, D. (1993), 'General Discussion', *Economic Policy*, no.17: 350–2.

Rowland, R.H. (1988), 'Union Migration Trends in the USSR during the 1980s', *Soviet Geography*, November: 809–29.

Rumer, B. (1983), 'The Regional Structure of Investment and Development of Soviet Industry: Tendencies and Contradictions', *Jahrbuch der Wirtschaft Osteuropas*, pp. 207–39.

Sachs, J. and A. Warner (1995), 'Economic Reform and the Process of Global Integration', *Brookings Papers on Economic Activity*, no.1: pp.1–118.

Sala-i-Martin, X. and J. Sachs (1991), 'Fiscal Federalism and Optimum Currency Areas: Evidence for Europe from the United States', *NBER Working Paper*, no.3855.

Schiffer, J.R. (1989), *Regional Economic Policy: The East-West debate over Pacific Siberian Development*, Macmillan, London.

Schroeder, G.E. (1994), 'Observations on Economic Reform in the Soviet Successor States', *Post Soviet Geography*, no.1: 1–13.

Schwarz, L. (1991), 'USSR Nationality Redistribution by Republic, 1979–1989: From Published Results of the 1989 All-Union Census', *Soviet Geography*, September: 209–48.

Scitovsky, T. (1958), *Economic Theory and West European Integration*, Allen and Unwin, Stanford, CA.

Selm, G. van (1995a), 'Integration and Disintegration in Europe: EC versus Former USSR', in B. Dallago and G. Pegoretti eds, *Integration and Disintegration in Europe: Convergent or Divergent Processes*, Dartmouth, Aldershot, pp. 93–111.

—— (1995b), 'A Gravity Model of the Former Soviet Union', *Journal of International and Comparative Economics*, no.1: 61–9.

—— (1995c), 'The Economics of Soviet Breakup', *Ukrainian Economic Review*, no.1–2: 80–95.

Selm, G. van and E. Dölle (1993), 'Soviet Interrepublican Capital Transfers

151

and the Republics' Level of Development 1966–91', *MOST. Economic Journal on Eastern Europe and the Former Soviet Union*, no.1: 133–49.

Selm, G. van and H.J. Wagener (1993), 'Soviet Republics' Economic Interdependence', *Osteuropa Wirtschaft*, no.1: 23–40.

Shamshur, O. (1993), 'Current Crisis and Migrations in the Former USSR', Paper presented at the NATO Colloquium, Brussels.

Smit, H. and V. Pechota eds (1994), *Privatisation in Eastern Europe: Legal, Economic and Social Aspects*, Martinus Nijhoff, Dordrecht.

Smith, Adam (1976), *An Enquiry into the Nature and Causes of the Wealth of Nations*, Oxford (original 1776).

Smith, Alan (1995), 'Trade and Payments between the former Soviet Republics', in A. Smith ed., *Challenges for Russian Economic Reform*, Royal Institute of International Affairs, London, pp.203–65.

Svoboda, V. (1992), 'Was the Soviet Union Really Necessary?', *Soviet Studies*, vol.44, no.5: 761–84.

Swann, D. (1988), *The Economics of the Common Market*, Penguin, London.

Tedstrom, J.E. (1995), 'Ukraine: A Crash Course in Economic Transition', *Comparative Economic Studies*, vol.37, no.4: 49–67.

Theil, H. (1967), *Economics and Information Theory*, North-Holland, Chicago.

Tinbergen, J. *et al.* (1962), *Shaping the World Economy: Suggestions for an International Economic Policy*, Twentieth Century Fund, New York.

Treml, V.G. *et al.* (1972), *The Structure of the Soviet Economy. Analysis and Reconstruction of the 1966 Input-Output Table*, Praeger, New York.

United Nations (1990), *1988 International Trade Statistics Yearbook*, vol.2: Trade by commodity, New York.

Vanous, J. (1992), *Plan Econ Report*, vol. 8, no.11–13, Washington, DC.

—— (1994), *Plan Econ Report*, April 28, Washington, DC.

Viner, J. (1950), *The Customs Union Issue*, Carnegie Endowment for International Peace, London.

Vjugin, O and A. Vavilov (1992), *Trade Patterns of Soviet Republics after Integration in the World Economy*, manuscript.

Wagener, H.-J. (1972), *Wirtschaftswachstum in unterentwickelten Gebieten: Ansätze zu einer Regionalanalyse der Sowjetunion*, Duncker & Humblot, Berlin.

—— (1973), 'Rules of Location and the Concept of Rationality: The case of the USSR', in V.N. Bandera and Z.L. Melnyk eds, *The Soviet Economy in Regional Perspective*, Praeger, New York, ch.3.

—— (1986), 'The Political Economy of Soviet Nationalities and Regions', in H. Höhmann *et al.* eds, *Economics and Politics in the USSR*, Westview Press, Boulder, CO, pp. 146–71.

Wagener, H.-J. and G. van Selm (1993), 'Soviet Regional Disintegration and Monetary Problems', *Communist Economies and Economic Transformation*, vol.5, no.4: 411–26.

Wang, Z.K. and L.A. Winters (1992), *The Trading Potential of Eastern Europe*, manuscript.

Williamson, J. (1992), 'Trade and Payments after Soviet Disintegration', *Policy Analyses in International Economics*, no.37, Washington, DC.

World Bank (1991), *World Development Report 1991*, New York.

—— (1992), *Statistical Handbook. States of the Former USSR*, Washington, DC.

INDEX